Racing with Heroes

Heroes

The stories, settings and characters from some of the most thrilling and iconic motor races between 1935 and 2011

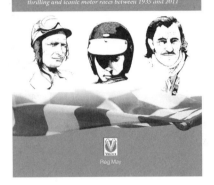

Reg May

T0386636

Also from Veloce Publishing ...

RAC handbooks
Caring for your car – How to maintain & service your car (Fry)
Caring for your car's bodywork and interior (Nixon)
Caring for your bicycle – How to maintain & repair your bicycle (Henshaw)
How your motorcycle works – Your guide to the components & systems of modern motorcycles (Henshaw)
Caring for your scooter – How to maintain & service your 49cc to 125cc twist & go scooter (Fry)
Efficient Driver's Handbook, The (Moss)
Electric Cars – The Future is Now! (Linde)
First aid for your car – Your expert guide to common problems & how to fix them (Collins)
How your car works (Linde)
Motorcycles – A first-time-buyer's guide (Henshaw)
Motorhomes – A first-time-buyer's guide (Fry)
Pass the MoT test! – How to check & prepare your car for the annual MoT test (Paxton)
Selling your car – How to make your car look great and how to sell it fast (Knight)
Simple fixes for your car – How to do small jobs for yourself and save money (Collins)

Those Were The Days ... Series
Alpine Trials & Rallies 1910-1973 (Pfundner)
Brighton National Speed Trials (Gardiner)
British and European Trucks of the 1970s (Peck)
British Drag Racing – The early years (Pettitt)
British Touring Car Racing (Collins)
Café Racer Phenomenon, The (Walker)
Drag Bike Racing in Britain – From the mid '60s to the mid '80s (Lee)
Endurance Racing at Silverstone in the 1970s & 1980s (Parker)
Hot Rod & Stock Car Racing in Britain in the 1980s (Neil)
Last Real Austins 1946-1959, The (Peck)
MG's Abingdon Factory (Moylan)
Motor Racing at Brands Hatch in the Seventies (Parker)
Motor Racing at Brands Hatch in the Eighties (Parker)
Motor Racing at Crystal Palace (Collins)
Motor Racing at Goodwood in the Sixties (Gardiner)
Motor Racing at Nassau in the 1950s & 1960s (O'Neil)
Motor Racing at Oulton Park in the 1960s (McFadyen)
Motor Racing at Oulton Park in the 1970s (McFadyen)
Motor Racing at Thruxton in the 1970s (Grant-Braham)
Motor Racing at Thruxton in the 1980s (Grant-Braham)
Superprix – The Story of Birmingham Motor Race (Page & Collins)

Biographies
Amédée Gordini ... a true racing legend (Smith)
André Lefebvre, and the cars he created at Voisin and Citroën (Beck)
Cliff Allison, The Official Biography of – From the Fells to Ferrari (Gauld)
Edward Turner – The Man Behind the Motorcycles (Clew)
Jack Sears, The Official Biography of – Gentleman Jack (Gauld)
Jim Redman – 6 Times World Motorcycle Champion: The Autobiography (Redman)
John Chatham – 'Mr Big Healey' – The Official Biography (Burr)
Lee Noble Story, The (Wilkins)
Pat Moss Carlsson Story, The – Harnessing Horsepower (Turner)
Tony Robinson – The biography of a race mechanic (Wagstaff)
Virgil Exner – Visioneer: The Official Biography of Virgil M Exner Designer Extraordinaire (Grist)

General
1½-litre GP Racing 1961-1965 (Whitelock)
AC Two-litre Saloons & Buckland Sportscars (Archibald)
Alfa Romeo 155/156/147 Competition Touring Cars (Collins)
Alfa Romeo Giulia Coupé GT & GTA (Tipler)
Alfa Romeo Montreal – The dream car that came true (Taylor)
Alfa Romeo Montreal – The Essential Companion (Taylor)
Alfa Tipo 33 (McDonough & Collins)
Alpine & Renault – The Development of the Revolutionary Turbo F1 Car 1968 to 1979 (Smith)
Alpine & Renault – The Sports Prototypes 1963 to 1969 (Smith)
Alpine & Renault – The Sports Prototypes 1973 to 1978 (Smith)
Anatomy of the Works Minis (Moylan)
Armstrong-Siddeley (Smith)
Autodrome (Collins & Ireland)
Autodrome 2 (Collins & Ireland)
Automotive A-Z, Lane's Dictionary of Automotive Terms (Lane)
Bahamas Speed Weeks, The (O'Neil)
Bentley Continental, Corniche and Azure (Bennett)
Bentley MkVI, Rolls-Royce Silver Wraith, Dawn & Cloud/Bentley R & S-Series (Nutland)
BMC Competitions Department Secrets (Turner, Chambers & Browning)
BMW 5-Series (Cranswick)
BMW Z-Cars (Taylor)
BMW Boxer Twins 1970-1995 Bible, The (Falloon)
BMW Custom Motorcycles – Choppers, Cruisers, Bobbers, Trikes & Quads (Cloesen)
BMW – The Power of M (Vivian)
Bonjour – Is this Italy? (Turner)
British at Indianapolis, The (Wagstaff)
British Cars, The Complete Catalogue of, 1895-1975 (Culshaw & Horrobin)
BRM – A Mechanic's Tale (Salmon)
BRM V16 (Ludvigsen)
Bugatti Type 40 (Price)
Bugatti 46/50 Updated Edition (Price & Arbey)
Bugatti T44 & T49 (Price & Arbey)
Bugatti 57 2nd Edition (Price)
Carrera Panamericana, La (Tipler)
Chrysler 300 – America's Most Powerful Car 2nd Edition (Ackerson)
Chrysler PT Cruiser (Ackerson)
Citroën DS (Bobbitt)
Classic British Car Electrical Systems (Astley)
Cobra – The Real Thing! (Legate)
Cortina – Ford's Bestseller (Robson)
Coventry Climax Racing Engines (Hammill)
Daily Mirror 1970 World Cup Rally 40, The (Robson)
Daimler SP250 New Edition (Long)
Datsun Fairlady Roadster to 280ZX – The Z-Car Story (Long)
Dino – The V6 Ferrari (Long)
Dodge Challenger & Plymouth Barracuda (Grist)
Dodge Charger – Enduring Thunder (Ackerson)
Dodge Dynamite! (Grist)
Drive on the Wild Side, A – 20 Extreme Driving Adventures From Around the World (Weaver)
Ducati 750 Bible, The (Falloon)
Ducati 750 SS 'round-case' 1974, The Book of the (Falloon)
Ducati 860, 900 and Mille Bible, The (Falloon)
Ducati Monster Bible, The (Falloon)
Fast Ladies – Female Racing Drivers 1888 to 1970 (Bouzanquet)
Fate of the Sleeping Beauties, The (op de Weegh/Hottendorff/op de Weegh)
Ferrari 288 GTO, The Book of the (Sackey)
Fiat & Abarth 124 Spider & Coupé (Tipler)
Fiat & Abarth 500 & 600 – 2nd Edition (Bobbitt)
Fiats, Great Small (Ward)
Ford Cleveland 335-Series V8 engine 1970 to 1982 – The Essential Source Book (Hammill)

Ford F100/F150 Pick-up 1948-1996 (Ackerson)
Ford GT – Then, and Now (Streather)
Ford GT40 (Legate)
Ford Thunderbird From 1954, The Book (Ackerson)
Formula 5000 Motor Racing, Back then ... and back now (Lawson)
Forza Minardi! (Vigar)
Funky Mopeds (Skelton)
GT – The World's Best GT Cars 1953-73 (Dawson)
Hillclimbing & Sprinting – The Essential Manual (Short & Wilkinson)
Honda NSX (Long)
Intermeccanica – The Story of the Prancing Bull (McCredie & Reisner)
Italian Custom Motorcycles (Cloesen)
Jaguar, The Rise of (Price)
Jaguar XJ 220 – The Inside Story (Moreton)
Jaguar XJ-S, The Book of the (Long)
Karmann-Ghia Coupé & Convertible (Bobbitt)
Kawasaki Triples Bible, The (Walker)
Kris Meeke – Intercontinental Rally Challenge Champion (McBride)
Lamborghini Miura Bible, The (Sackey)
Lamborghini Urraco, The Book of the (Landsem)
Lambretta Bible, The (Davies)
Lancia 037 (Collins)
Lancia Delta HF Integrale (Blaettel & Wagner)
Land Rover Series III Reborn (Porter)
Land Rover, The Half-ton Military (Cook)
Laverda Twins & Triples Bible 1968-1986 (Falloon)
Lea-Francis Story, The (Price)
Le Mans Panoramic (Ireland)
Lexus Story, The (Long)
Lola – The Illustrated History (1957-1977) (Starkey)
Lola – All the Sports Racing & Single-seater Racing Cars 1978-1997 (Starkey)
Lola T70 – The Racing History & Individual Chassis Record – 4th Edition (Starkey)
Lotus 49 (Oliver)
Mazda MX-5/Miata 1.6 Enthusiast's Workshop Manual (Grainger & Shoemark)
Mazda MX-5/Miata 1.8 Enthusiast's Workshop Manual (Grainger & Shoemark)
Mazda MX-5 Miata: The Book of the World's Favourite Sportscar (Long)
Mazda MX-5 Miata Roadster (Long)
Maximum Mini (Booij)
Mercedes-Benz SL – W113-series 1963-1971 (Long)
Mercedes-Benz SL & SLC – 107-series 1971-1989 (Long)
MGA (Price Williams)
MGB & MGB GT– Expert Guide (Auto-doc Series) (Williams)
MGB Electrical Systems Updated & Revised Edition (Astley)
Mini Cooper – The Real Thing! (Tipler)
Mini Minor to Asia Minor (West)
Mitsubishi Lancer Evo, The Road Car & WRC Story (Long)
Montlhery, The Story of the Paris Autodrome (Boddy)
Morgan Maverick (Lawrence)
Morris Minor, 60 Years on the Road (Newell)
Moto Guzzi Sport & Le Mans Bible, The (Falloon)
Motor Movies – The Posters! (Veysey)
Motor Racing – Reflections of a Lost Era (Carter)
Motor Racing – The Pursuit of Victory 1930-1962 (Carter)
Motor Racing – The Pursuit of Victory 1963-1972 (Wyatt/Sears)
Motorsport In colour, 1950s (Wainwright)
MV Agusta Fours, The book of the classic (Falloon)
Nissan 300ZX & 350Z – The Z-Car Story (Long)
Nissan GT-R Supercar: Born to race (Gorodji)
Northeast American Sports Car Races 1950-1959 (O'Neil)
Nothing Runs – Misadventures in the Classic, Collectable & Exotic Car Biz (Slutsky)
Off-Road Giants! (Volume 1) – Heroes of

1960s Motorcycle Sport (Westlake)
Off-Road Giants! (Volume 2) – Heroes of 1960s Motorcycle Sport (Westlake)
Pass the Theory and Practical Driving Tests (Gibson & Hoole)
Peking to Paris 2007 (Young)
Pontiac Firebird (Cranswick)
Porsche Boxster (Long)
Porsche 356 (2nd Edition) (Long)
Porsche 908 (Födisch, Neßhöver, Roßbach, Schwarz & Roßbach)
Porsche 911 Carrera – The Last of the Evolution (Corlett)
Porsche 911R, RS & RSR, 4th Edition (Starkey)
Porsche 911, The Book of the (Long)
Porsche 911SC 'Super Carrera' – The Essential Companion (Streather)
Porsche 914 & 914-6: The Definitive History of the Road & Competition Cars (Long)
Porsche 924 (Long)
Porsche 928 (Long)
Porsche 944 (Long)
Porsche 964, 993 & 996 Data Plate Code Breaker (Streather)
Porsche 993 'King Of Porsche' – The Essential Companion (Streather)
Porsche 996 'Supreme Porsche' – The Essential Companion (Streather)
Porsche Racing Cars – 1953 to 1975 (Long)
Porsche Racing Cars – 1976 to 2005 (Long)
Porsche – The Rally Story (Meredith)
Porsche: Three Generations of Genius (Meredith)
Preston Tucker & Others (Linde)
RAC Rally Action! (Gardiner)
Rallye Sport Fords: The Inside Story (Moreton)
Roads with a View – England's greatest views and how to find them by road (Corfield)
Roads With a View – Wales' greatest views and how to find them by road (Corfield)
Rolls-Royce Silver Shadow/Bentley T Series Corniche & Camargue – Revised & Enlarged Edition (Bobbitt)
Rolls-Royce Silver Spirit, Silver Spur & Bentley Mulsanne 2nd Edition (Bobbitt)
Runways & Racers (O'Neil)
RX-7 – Mazda's Rotary Engine Sportscar (Updated & Revised New Edition) (Long)
Singer Story: Cars, Commercial Vehicles, Bicycles & Motorcycle (Atkinson)
Sleeping Beauties USA – abandoned classic cars & trucks (Marek)
SM – Citroën's Maserati-engined Supercar (Long & Claverol)
Speedway – Auto racing's ghost tracks (Collins & Ireland)
Sprite Caravans, The Story of (Jenkinson)
Standard Motor Company, The Book of the (Robson)
Subaru Impreza: The Road Car And WRC Story (Long)
Supercar, How to Build your own (Thompson)
Tales from the Toolbox (Oliver)
Toleman Story, The (Hilton)
Toyota Celica & Supra, The Book of Toyota's Sports Coupés (Long)
Toyota MR2 Coupés & Spyders (Long)
Triumph Speed Twin & Thunderbird Bible (Woolridge)
Triumph Tiger Cub Bible (Estall)
Triumph Trophy Bible (Woolridge)
Triumph TR6 (Kimberley)
TWR Story, The – Group A (Hughes & Scott)
Unraced (Collins)
Velocette Motorcycles – MSS to Thruxton – New Third Edition (Burris)
Volkswagens of the World (Glen)
VW Beetle Cabriolet – The full story of the convertible Beetle (Bobbitt)
VW Beetle – The Car of the 20th Century (Copping)
VW Golf: Five Generations of Fun (Copping & Cservenka)
VW – The Air-cooled Era (Copping)
Which Oil? – Choosing the right oils & greases for your antique, vintage, veteran, classic or collector car (Michell)
Works Minis, The Last (Purves & Brenchley)
Works Rally Mechanic (Moylan)

www.veloce.co.uk

First published in November 2013 by Veloce Publishing Limited, Veloce House, Parkway Farm Business Park, Middle Farm Way, Poundbury, Dorchester, Dorset, DT1 3AR, England. Fax 01305 250479/e-mail info@veloce.co.uk/web www.veloce.co.uk or www.velocebooks.com.

ISBN: 978-1-845846-54-1   UPC: 6-36847-04654-5

Readers with ideas for automotive books, or books on other transport or related hobby subjects, are invited to write to the editorial director of Veloce Publishing at the above address.
British Library Cataloguing in Publication Data – A catalogue record for this book is available from the British Library.
Typesetting, design and page make-up all by Veloce Publishing Ltd on Apple Mac. Printed in India by Replika Press.

Racing with Heroes

The stories, settings and characters from some of the most thrilling and iconic motor races between 1935 and 2011

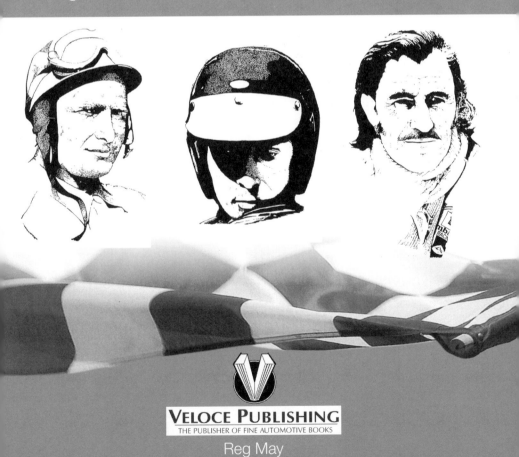

V

VELOCE PUBLISHING
THE PUBLISHER OF FINE AUTOMOTIVE BOOKS

Reg May

THIS BOOK IS DEDICATED TO

Grand Prix of England, Aintree 1955.
The winner Stirling Moss driving
his Mercedes-Benz W196

Sir Stirling Moss

With gratitude for his words of encouragement, which not only helped
me to complete this book, but also demonstrate the sincerity and
approachability of the man. One who can only be held in the highest esteem
as being a great driver, sportsman, ambassador and human being.

A true knight in shining armour.

CONTENTS

ACKNOWLEDGEMENTS 6
PREFACE. 7
INTRODUCTION 9

1 A PASSION FOR RACING 12
2 GERMAN GRAND PRIX – 1957 18
3 MONACO GRAND PRIX – 1961 25
4 LE MANS – 1969 31
5 BRAZILIAN GRAND PRIX – 2008. 37
6 FRENCH GRAND PRIX – 1959. 43
7 MILLE MIGLIA – 1955 49
8 GERMAN GRAND PRIX – 1935 58
9 ITALIAN GRAND PRIX – 1971 62
10 BRITISH GRAND PRIX – 1976 83
11 FRENCH GRAND PRIX – 1961 88
12 DUTCH GRAND PRIX – 1967 93
13 AUSTRALIAN GRAND PRIX – 1986 97
14 A FAMILY DAY AT THE RACES 101
15 CANADIAN GRAND PRIX – 2011 108
16 JAPANESE GRAND PRIX – 1976 114
17 HE RACED WITH HEROES 119

INDEX 127

ACKNOWLEDGEMENTS

Motor Sport	Published by Haymarket Publications
Motor Racing	Published by Pearl Cooper Ltd
Dicing with Death	Published by Daily Mirror Newspapers Ltd
In the Track of Speed	Published by Frederick Muller Ltd
The Motor Reference Year Book	Published by Temple Press Ltd
A Story of Formula 1	Published by Grenville Publishing Co Ltd
Motor Racing Year 1961	Published by Knightsbridge Group of Publications Ltd
Fangio My Racing Life	Published by Patrick Stephens Ltd
Illustrations	By Philip J May
Circuit Maps	By Philip J May
The Worst Act of Cheating ...	Times Newspaper / Simon Barnes
Bob Cook photographs	Bob Cook
Additional photographs	Julian Nowell

PREFACE

A T the outset I wish to make it clear that I have written this book purely as an enthusiastic motor racing fan. I am not a journalist, technical expert, driver or manager within the sport.

I have put pen to paper to record races from 1935 up to 2011 and have included such classics as the 1955 Mille Miglia and the 1957 German Grand Prix. Races that I have heard of and read about since my childhood. Races, drivers, circuits and teams that have left an impression on me over the years, and left me with a bug that has lasted ever since.

The author with Stirling Moss.

Also included within this book are some personal opinions, observations and reflections on motor racing in general and my own personal experiences of the sport. The book is intended to excite as well as inform the reader. To make the reader feel that he/she is there amidst the sights and sounds of those history making events, hence the title Racing With Heroes.

I believe I have injected some of my own enthusiasm for the sport, while endeavouring to paint as vivid a picture of each event and it's backdrop as possible for the reader to capture the atmosphere, so that he/she can enjoy reading about them as much as I have enjoyed writing about them.

The author with Stirling Moss and Martin Brundle.

INTRODUCTION

HOW IT ALL BEGAN

I was eleven years old at the time of my first trip to a motor racing circuit in 1958, and I can still remember that childish excitement to this day. Crystal Palace was the venue, a track that, for safety reasons, is sadly no longer used for motor racing events. The circuit was set in the shadow of the nearby giant radio mast in the south London park, and was home to all sorts of club, as well as international, races.

I was taken by Dennis, my elder brother, who, like me, had not seen a live motor race before. We had caught a London double-decker bus from our home in Bow in the East End of London to make our way to the circuit – an adventure of its own, as we passed through the Blackwall Tunnel into hitherto previously unknown territory. Luckily, the park was not too far from the bus stop where we alighted, after the conductor told us that this was the stop we needed. We made our way, following the more experienced shooting-stick and hamper-toting racegoers, towards the noise that we could already hear reverberating in our direction.

We bought a programme on the way, and to my amazement there were not one but seven races scheduled for that day. Looking through the programme there were many things that I did not understand. What were flags used for; why were there different classes of cars? There were car names and driver's names that I had never heard before. And what was that strange smell? In the course of that afternoon we witnessed cars of all shapes and sizes, from large Jaguar sports cars to rear-engined 500cc single-seaters that were powered by motorbike engines, as well as touring cars that one could see on the roads every day.

The biggest problem for two young boys was trying to find the best vantage point to be able to see. Unfortunately, the place with the best view was not the closest, and I wanted to be close enough to touch, to see the look on the drivers' faces, to feel the vibration as they went past, and to breathe in that rich, hot oil and rubber smell that effused whenever they went by. In short, I wanted to be part of it.

The public address system would blare out its information about the changing fortunes of the cars and drivers throughout the races. Not that you could make much

Racing with Heroes

sense of it above the roar of the engines and screeching of the tyres as the cars passed by. Consequently, that commentary which was discernible was somewhat disjointed, and the only way to follow the race was by constantly referring to the race programme for driver name, car type, and its number. Things haven't changed much (big screens excepted).

In-between races as we looked around us, we could see the seasoned racegoers taking it easy in collapsible chairs or on picnic blankets spread on the ground. Some were tucking in to hampers of sandwiches and cakes, flasks of tea, or even the odd bottle of something a bit stronger. This was a world that we hadn't seen before.

From time to time I was to return to Crystal Palace with school friends, family, and Marie, my 'wife-to-be', in the years to come. At one such meeting I was privileged to witness a virtuoso performance by a virtually unknown Austrian driver by the name of Jochen Rindt. It was plain to see that here was a star of the future. We didn't know at that time that he would fulfil his ambition of becoming World Champion, or that he would unfortunately become the first posthumous World Champion, following his fatal crash at Monza.

In the meantime, Crystal Palace was followed by trips to Brands Hatch, Goodwood, and later, Silverstone. My passion had now been kindled, and an idol had appeared. Stirling Moss seemed to encapsulate all that appealed to me, especially after reading some of his biographies. Race reports such as that of the 1955 Mille Miglia also made a deep impression on me. There are a number of references within these pages to Sir Stirling Moss (as he is now). For this I make no apology, as he is often considered by many (myself included) to be the greatest British driver of all time, and one who is generally respected by his peers and the racing community as a whole.

As I grew older I went to see the British Grand Prix and The Race of Champions, and then ventured further afield to Zandvoort and Monte Carlo to see the Grands Prix. The trip to Monaco was a once-in-a-lifetime, never-to-be-forgotten experience, during which we met and talked to Sir Stirling Moss and Martin Brundle, the whole thing being organized to perfection by Grand Prix Adventures Ltd.

For a period I joined the BRSCC (British Racing & Sports Car Club), and became a marshal. At this stage, my eldest son was now old enough to come with me. We attended club meetings, Formula Ford Festivals, 1000 kilometre sports car races; as well as the British Grand Prix at Brands Hatch, and some very enjoyable nights at the Kentagon, courtesy of the BRSCC.

The passion has not diminished over the years. Champions have come and gone: Brabham, Clark, Hill, Surtees, Ickx, Bell, Stewart, Rindt, Lauda, Hunt, Rosberg, Piquet, Prost, Senna, Mansell, Schumacher, Alonso, etc, some of whom are no longer with us. Some great teams have also disappeared such as Maserati, Vanwall, Cooper, BRM, Lotus, Alfa Romeo, and Brabham. Manufacturers like Maserati and Alfa Romeo may return in the future, but the small private companies are probably lost forever. Unfortunately that is the way of things, and I am sure new ones will take their place.

Many would argue that motor racing, particularly Formula 1, is not what it used to be. There is some truth in this, but motor racing is a highly technological sport, and as such is ever-changing, perhaps not always the way we would wish. Technical advances of car/engine design seem now to make a greater difference than driver ability. Having said that, there will always be a handful of drivers at any period in time whose prowess behind the wheel will make them stand out from the rest. It is also now possible to 'coach' drivers from the pits via two-way radios, instead of simply being advised of the race situation by means of pit boards. Sportsmanship of some individual drivers who should have known better has also been called into doubt in recent years. Probably the main difference now, however, is the financial approach to racing with sponsorship for drivers, as well as the teams forming an essential part of the scene.

In truth, I feel that the halcyon days are past. It seems that motor racing is now a big business rather than a sport; hijacked by the 'professionals,' entrepreneurs, television companies, and manufacturers. Jackie Stewart wanted the sport to be more professional for the best of reasons, namely safety. Who could argue with that? To achieve his fastest lap a driver can drive as fast as he can until he runs out of road or ability, to bounce across a kerb or onto a run-off area, then he knows that he has reached his limit without fear of his progress being halted by a tree or telegraph pole or earth bank. Improvements in safety have largely been achieved, but the cost is that parts of many circuits are now only defined by white lines; spectators are separated from the track by ever-growing expanses of run-off areas.

It is now very difficult to identify the drivers once they are ensconced in their machines, let alone see their faces or study their driving style. For television purposes it seems Grands Prix are now about the same duration as a football match, which makes one wonder how the likes of Lewis Hamilton or Michael Schumacher would get by in the Mille Miglia. Rules and regulations are added to, or tinkered with, on an almost ad hoc basis – to manufacture a good race for the television viewers, to ensure television coverage, and thus maintain the income. How long will it be before the race results are decided by Simon Cowell and a viewer's phone vote? Or am I becoming cynical in my old age?

1 A PASSION FOR RACING

PEOPLE can have a passion for many things. Drivers such as Fangio, Moss, Clark, Surtees, Andretti, and Bell, to name but a few, have a passion for racing by the bucketful – it is in their every fibre. No matter what type of car, what type of event, what type of weather and what type of circuit, they will answer the challenge and race. They are of a certain breed. The money, fame and lifestyle are secondary to their passion for racing.

It is not only the drivers but also the likes of Colin Chapman, Ron Dennis, Ken Tyrrell, Rob Walker, Denis Jenkinson, Raymond Mays, Alf Francis; all had, and have, that same passion. Whatever their position, whether it be driver, team owner, journalist, or mechanic, it's in their blood, and it is something they cannot do without.

Ever since the early days of motoring, man has wanted to pit himself together with his machine against other men with their machines, to prove that he and his machine are faster. Whether it be from point A to point B, as in the early city-to-city races, or on specially designed circuits, the challenge has been the same from France to Australia; from the United States of America to China. There is hardly a place on the globe where the sport does not make its presence felt.

In the early days of racing there was no such thing as a professional. It was largely a hobby for the rich, but even so the likes of Jenatzy, Malcolm Campbell, Lautenschlager, and Seagrave all wanted to create new records and frontiers, and to break new ground.

Many have paid for their passion with their lives, but for all those involved, the risk is all part of the passion, and without the risk there would be no passion.

Some drivers, even great drivers, like James Hunt and Jackie Stewart, have been able to hang up their helmet and walk away, never to race again. This shows great determination, but one cannot help but wonder how often would they have liked just one more race. For people like Stirling Moss and Niki Lauda following their horrific accidents, perhaps the choice was easier, but even until very recently Moss still liked to get back behind the wheel whenever he could, at events such as the Goodwood Revival meetings. Niki Lauda still has strong links with Grand Prix racing, and even Schumacher has, since retiring at the end of the 2007 season, returned to the world of Formula 1 after experimenting with the two-wheeled variety of racing machine.

One only has to look at the mass migration to Le Mans each year where the spectators will endure the noise, the weather and the discomfort – many under canvas during the twenty-four hours, not to mention the hours endured travelling to and from the circuit – to see that this passion for motor racing is not confined only to those directly involved.

Quite often, as in the case of Alberto Ascari and Jacques Villeneuve, the love of the sport is passed on through the family. Ascari's father, Antonio, was a famous driver for Alfa Romeo who was unfortunately killed when Alberto was still quite young. As a child, Alberto was surrounded by the constant talk and atmosphere of racing, and no doubt on occasions found himself in the company of his father's racing colleagues and associates.

The passion can be inspired by the speed, competition, money, glamour, patriotic fervour, technical fascination, or the atmosphere. It can be any one of these, or a combination of some or indeed all of these factors. There have already been a great number of books written on the subject, and possibly millions have been bought and read. This is just one more, but in this instance penned by a passionate fan rather than a 'super-scribe' or technical expert.

At the beginning of the twenty-first century things are somewhat different to how they were at the beginning of the twentieth century. Huge amounts of money can now be earned and spent in the course of a single season, which certainly was not the case in 1906, when cars and competition motoring were in their infancy. Winning can be very prestigious both for the driver and the car manufacturer. Drivers such as Senna, Fangio and Nuvolari, to name but three, have immortalised themselves not just in their own countries but throughout the motoring world. Songs have been written about them, statues erected to them, even museums commissioned to laud their achievements.

How could Niki Lauda have hauled himself from what was believed to have literally been his deathbed after receiving the Last Rites following that terrible accident in 1976 to drive some six weeks later in the Italian Grand Prix, if he had not been driven by a passionate desire to race again? How could Nuvolari sit on his motor bike again to race in 1922 after having just discharged himself from the hospital, still in plaster, and ask friends to place him onto his 350cc machine if he did not have the fire and passion within him to do so? How could Alex Zanardi rise to the challenge of racing again after having lost both his legs in that terrifying crash at Lausitzring in Germany while taking part in a CART Champcar race in 2001, without that burning desire? To some, this sort of thing is incomprehensible and irresponsible, but to these people and many others like them it is their life, their whole raison d'être.

Motorsport at one time was a plaything only for the rich; to a degree this is still true. Today, certainly at the top level of Formula 1, millions if not billions of pounds are swashing around within the sport to pay for drivers, teams, circuits, advertising, television rights, etc. It was always considered a glamorous sport for the drivers and the entrants but for the likes of mechanics, journalists and support teams it has not always been so. You will see teams of a dozen or more pit crew all dressed in the team corporate uniforms, the colours of their sponsors, or in looking like something from a sci-fi film or

Racing with Heroes

NASA crew, but you need only go back as far as the '60s to see grease-marked overalled mechanics carrying churns and funnels to refuel a car in the pits, or carrying a large hammer to remove the knock-off hub caps for a quick wheel change. The 'removal lorries', or coaches fitted-out to transport the cars and spares of that era have now been replaced by large exotic transporters, motor homes/hospitality offices – complete with kitchens, computers, and telemetry equipment. No longer do the mechanics recount their stories of getting to race tracks around Europe by hitching a lift with the team transporter, or of trying to find a hotel room for race weekend. Yes, the mechanics will still work long hours repairing a car after their driver had misjudged a corner or braking point, but as I write this, plans are afoot to limit the hours that mechanics may work on a car .

Denis Jenkinson would trundle around Europe in his trusty Porsche 911, meeting up with the likes of Innes Ireland, David Piper, and other colleagues on his way to the various circuits, finding some of the quieter spots to spend a pleasant afternoon or evening with an accompanying glass of wine to discuss the more weighty matters of the world, such as the forthcoming race, pretty girls, or the next bottle of wine. To some degree this may not have changed very much, but I feel sure that, as in most other aspects of today's world, time is money; sponsors, promoters, TV companies – all want their pound of flesh, and there is less opportunity for the social side than there used to be.

Recently, dissatisfaction has been expressed by the viewing fans, the drivers, the teams, and the FIA, as well as Bernie Ecclestone, regarding the lack of overtaking, the inability of drivers to get close to another car, the dominance of a team or driver; all of which, it is claimed, has led to boring processional races. None of which is good for attracting new fans, for keeping the current ones happy, or selling the sport as a spectacle to television companies. To combat this, many changes to the rules have been introduced in recent years, such as the banning of traction control, compulsory pit stops, and grooved tyres. Unfortunately, the majority of these measures do not address the main problem: allowing the cars to get close enough for the drivers to race each other. This has been a problem since the advent of wings and the ground effect aerodynamic designs of the cars' chassis, which requires them to run in clean air to get the full downforce needed them to handle at their best. As a result, if two cars are close together when approaching a corner, the second car will lose downforce and will either understeer off the track, or the driver will have to back off and lose any chance, at that corner at least, of overtaking.

Dominant drivers and teams will always arise, for a time, before they are deposed – take the likes of Ascari, Fangio, Clark, Senna, Schumacher, not to mention Sebastian Vettel, for example. For a driver to even reach the top levels of the sport – be it Formula 1, sports car racing, or indeed almost any category – a driver has to be single-minded and dedicated, in most cases from a very early age (although some late starters have made it through, a good example was Graham Hill – one of the most respected and successful drivers of all time. Even the great Fangio did not enter into Grand Prix racing until he was 38 in 1949, although he did his apprenticeship driving saloon cars in local South American races from the age of 25).

A Passion for Racing

As for the teams, Mercedes-Benz, McLaren, Lotus, Cooper, Maserati, Ferrari, Alfa Romeo, Williams, Jaguar, Audi, Bugatti, Renault, Vanwall, BRM – and I am sure there are more – all have, for greater or lesser periods, dominated the sport at one time or another.

From a relatively early age my passion for motor racing was fuelled by reading the likes of *Autocar* and *Motor*; this progressed to *MotorSport,* then *Motor Racing,* and later *Autosport.* It was no doubt after reading Denis Jenkinson's wonderful race reports in *MotorSport* that I invested twenty five shillings of my hard-earned paper round wages in a copy of *A Story of Formula One,* which I have read a number of times and, although now slightly battered, it is still a cherished item on my bookshelf.

My passion was further fired by watching the televised Grands Prix that were shown over the Eurovision link in the early days of satellite communication, and commentated on by the knowledgeable and assured voice of Raymond Baxter before the days of 'hype TV' and screaming commentators. Quite often these transmissions were confined to only short 15-30min airings that would show the start and finish of the events: if there happened to be a delay in the start then they would run out of time and the transmission slot would be lost. But even in those monochrome days there was still something magical about seeing those iconic names of racing: Brabham, Moss, Salvadori, McLaren, Clark, Hill, Ireland, Surtees, Gurney, Bueb, Behra, Schell, and their contemporaries.

Another highlight for me was the twenty-four hour race at Le Mans, during which hourly reports would be transmitted by the BBC's Simon Taylor and John Bolster. I would listen to these throughout the Saturday afternoon and through the night, as well as the early hours of Sunday morning, on my small Japanese transistor radio with earpiece firmly in place. For all those involved in motorsport at whatever level, no matter how peripheral, there must always be the passion to be involved. This can be seen at no better level than that of the race marshals who largely carry out their work unpaid. They pay their own expenses, carry out their duties, often at great danger to their own safety, and put in many hours at the circuits for the events, as well as training and travelling to enable the race meetings to go ahead in the relative safety of a sport that is inherently dangerous to all those present. Having been involved with some of these people with the BRSCC at one stage while marshalling, one cannot help but have nothing but praise for these stalwarts of the sport, a number of whom have given their lives over the years that others may compete and watch their chosen sport feeling just that little bit more secure and comfortable, knowing that these people are on hand. I may be biased, but it's my opinion that we have in this country the best marshals, and this is proved by the fact that they are often invited to tender their services at international tracks and events.

It's not only the sights, but also the sounds and smells at a race meeting that, for me, elicit the excitement and passion, and I am sure I'm not the only one to be affected by this heady cocktail which starts the adrenaline coursing through one's veins. Whether it's the rumble of a low-revving V8, or the shriller, rasping note of a high-revving V12, it makes no difference. I know from his writings that Denis Jenkinson used to enjoy the sight of a Formula 1 car being driven on public roads (as often happened during the early

Racing with Heroes

days of the sport), by a mechanic taking the car from an overnight lock-up or garage to the nearby circuit – turning the heads of the passers by, particularly the children, as it went. A thoroughbred of the circuits making its way up the high street and through the traffic lights with all the other commuting and workaday vehicles is sadly pretty much a lost spectacle today. Another pleasurable sight and one that is often covered by the crop of artists such as Michael Turner and Alan Fearnely that are so popular now, was the sight of three or four Italian scarlet-, British racing green-, or German silver-liveried cars being readied, or just standing in the paddock prior to the main event of the day. Sometimes these paintings depict one or more of the drivers seated in them, making sure that everything was in place and working. Other scenes may see a flurry of activity on one of the cars, with mechanics buzzing around it like wasps around a nest. Or, all may be calm and tranquillity (if that is possible in a racing paddock), as the drivers and mechanics stand in small groups talking, joking, and laughing with one another, or perhaps discussing their chances in the race to come.

Because of my introduction to the sport in the late '50s, I find a trip to the Goodwood Speed Week very nostalgic and thought-provoking. The sight of those lovely old Lancias, Maseratis, BRMs, Lotus, Ferraris, Coopers, Aston Martins, Jaguars, etc, can transport me half a century back in time in the blink of an eye as my imagination runs wild. I can vividly see them once again on the grid, the packed stands hushed with expectation, the national flags fluttering in the wind; Fangio, Ascari, Moss, Brabham, Hill and Behra at the wheel, lowering their goggles, glancing around them, blipping the accelerator, and getting a feel for the clutch in anticipation of the flag about to fall. The engine notes rise, then suddenly the flag falls, the clutches are dropped, the rear wheels of 24 or more cars spin, and the rubber smoke pours off them (it would be another 40 years or more before traction control was introduced), and they are held for a split second in suspended animation. Suddenly the tyres grip, and as one the grid is on the move and thundering down to the first corner, jostling for position, the drivers' feet dancing on the pedals as they simultaneously brake and change gear to hustle the cars through the corner. Another blink, and I am back to reality, looking simply at a gleaming piece of history standing before me – but what a history!

Unfortunately, in recent years numerous incidents have tarnished what many consider to be the gem of the motorsporting crown that Formula 1 is meant to represent. Allegations of deliberately driving into another car, stealing another team's designs, or deliberately crashing to affect the race result. All this as the profile of Formula 1 has been raised to unprecedented levels through increased media exposure. Motor racing is a sport that thrives on technological advancement, but one cannot help but look to the past; when things were more primitive, but more sporting, and a camaraderie existed. Whether these latest developments have come about because the danger levels have been greatly reduced, whether it is because of the greater financial rewards, or whether it is symptomatic of the world we live in today is debatable. Technology may change, but the sportsmanship and the moral standards should remain the same, whether the racing takes place in 1912 or 2012. For if it does not, the sport will be that much poorer for it, and cease to be a sport – the passion simply to race lost forever.

2 GERMAN GRAND PRIX – 1957

THE PROLOGUE

NEARLY three-and-a-half hours after the fall of the flag to start the race at 1.15pm, the German Grand Prix was over ...

In a blur of colour, and a cacophony of sound, the drivers and their machines had torn through over fourteen miles of twists and turns that comprised every lap of the awe-inspiring circuit. A circuit that three times World Champion Jackie Stewart described as "The green hell."

For nearly three-and-a-half hours Fangio, Hawthorn, and Collins had participated in a monumental battle for supremacy from which, at the end of the day, Fangio emerged triumphant, not just proving the quality of his driving but also, if proof was needed, that he could drive with his head as well as his right foot.

The year was 1957, the date August 4, the place, the Nürburgring. Over fourteen miles of the most difficult road circuit in the world, with its 275 corners, bends and kinks, it was impossible to know it completely.

The track, which still exists today, is located in the picturesque setting of the Eifel Mountains. In the distance towers the brooding edifice that is the 12th century medieval Nürburg Castle, which is often shrouded in mist. Off to the west lie the Ardennes and Belgium; to the east is the Rhine, and below, in the very shadow of the castle, is the Nordschleife – part of the Nürburgring racing circuit.

It can be an intimidating place, especially when the weather closes in, as it is wont to do at certain times of the year: giving it that eerie, haunting atmosphere of a 1950s black and white movie, or a Wagner-inspired piece of music. With parts of the circuit having such atmospheric names as Hantzenbach, Hocheichen, Quiddelbacher Höhe, Flugplatz, Schwedencruez, and Karrusel, this is a place where you can almost feel the presence of past Teutonic heroes such as von Brauchitsch, Caracciola and Rosemeyer hurtling around in their thundering silver monsters at breakneck speeds, seemingly almost out of control, but always perfectly in command. Names inextricably linked with those of Mercedes-Benz, Auto Union, Neubauer, and Uhlenhaut; Titans of those prewar golden days of glory for Deutschland.

Originally during the 1920s, a series of races known as ADAC Eiffelrennen were run on the public roads of the Eifel mountains, but these were seen to be too dangerous and not practical. So it was decided to build a circuit like no other, as befits a world-leading nation.

Construction was started in 1925 during times of high unemployment by a 3000-strong construction team, and the track officially opened on June 18, 1927. It incorporated almost every natural and man-made hazard possible. The last race run on the full ring was in 1939; future races would be run on the slightly shorter Nordschleife circuit. The circuit facilities included an hotel, the paddock – which had 70 lockable garages, and the Continental control tower for timekeepers and race control. It was not until four years later that the electronic tracking result board was added. The first race to be given the title of the German Grand Prix took place in 1951. It is said that during the course of the European Grand Prix held there in 1954, more than 400,000 spectators attended.

The one particular hazard that makes the ring so difficult to master is the unpredictable weather. The length of the lap means that it can be dry on one part of the circuit, wet on another, and dry again further into the lap. This is also exacerbated by the areas of overhanging trees which keep the surface damp in patches. The lap is undulating, with the road rising and dipping almost continuously.

Ferrari had a particularly strong team in 1957, with two English drivers Mike Hawthorn and Peter Collins, as well as Luigi Musso driving for them. The cars were the latest 801 models, a derivative of the earlier Lancia version. Fangio and Behra were teamed up to drive Maserati 250Fs. Moss, Brooks and Stuart Lewis-Evans had arrived fresh from their success at the British Grand Prix with their Vanwalls. It would not be until the following year that these beautiful cars, produced by the wealthy industrialist Tony Vandervell, would fulfil his dream of forming a team to beat the best the Italian manufacturers could offer.

The remainder of the 26 car grid was made up from a number of Maseratis, driven by Harry Schell, Hans Hermann, Masten Gregory, Bruce Halford, Scarlatti, Godia and Gould. These were augmented by the Formula 2 Cooper Climaxes of Salvadori, Brabham, Naylor, Gibson, England and Marsh, as well as the Porsche RS Formula 2 cars driven by Barth, Maglioli and De Beaufort.

By this stage of the season Fangio had already won at Argentina, Monte Carlo and France, while Moss had won the British Grand Prix at Aintree, with only the Italian Grand Prix at Monza to follow in September. Unfortunately for Moss, Vanwalls were debuting at this circuit, so setting up the car's suspension was taking time ... if there was one circuit on the calendar where a driver needed the car to be set up correctly, this was it.

It looked like a straightforward fight between the two teams of red Italian cars – Ferrari v Maserati – with (on paper at least), Ferrari looking the stronger of the two. Fangio however could never be discounted, for at this stage of his career 'the old man' had already won four World Championships (1951, 1954, 1955 and 1956) and what's more, each one in a different make of car.

Racing with Heroes

PRACTICE

The weather was fine, the sun had dried the track from the recent rain: conditions were good.

The timekeeper's sheets during the first practice session on the Friday were headed by J M Fangio with a time of 9min 34sec. That was somewhat quicker than the previous year's lap time, partly explained by the fact that the circuit had been modified in places. But Fangio, being Fangio, did not leave it there: he went out again, and to everyone's amazement he scorched round in the unbelievable time of 9min 25.6sec. This was Fangio at his best.

Hawthorn at this point could only manage a time of 9min 37.8sec, and unfortunately he could not better this, no matter how much he hurled the Ferrari around the circuit. That is, until the second day of practice during which he really began to show his mettle and got within three seconds of Fangio's time by recording a lap time of 9min 28.5sec.

Meanwhile Moss, Brooks, and Lewis-Evans were having a miserable time. Owing to the team's lack of experience at the 'ring, they spent most of their time setting the cars up with the correct gear ratios, suspension adjustments etc. Their lap times reflected the buffeting that they were taking in the ill-handling Vanwalls, which themselves were showing signs of the stress being imposed on the chassis. It was not looking good for the team of green cars from England which had, in recent races, begun to show real promise, especially after their dominance at Aintree just weeks earlier. The mechanics were kept busy during the days – and in some instances the nights – prior to the race, constantly adjusting and readjusting gearings and settings on the cars in an effort to get the very best out of them.

By Sunday morning the talk in the bar of the Sporthotel at the circuit was whether Hawthorn would be able to spoil Fangio's bid for a hat-trick of wins at this venue, which was considered to be very much a driver's circuit.

It was known that the Maseratis intended to start the race with their fuel tanks only half-full and be running on the softer Pirelli tyres. This would allow them to get away quickly from the grid, but would require a pit stop at mid distance – thus putting the onus on the Ferraris to try to keep up with them.

To counter this strategy the Ferraris were to start with full tanks. Although this would make them slower off the line at the start, they hoped to be able to leap-frog the Maseratis during their pit stops for fuel and tyres at the halfway mark. The Ferraris would be running on the harder Englebert tyres, which would last the full race distance. It was therefore essential for Fangio to get a good start and make the most of his lighter fuel load during the early part of the race. It was equally important for the Ferrari team to stay in touch during those early laps.

It should be borne in mind that although the race was to be just over 310 miles in length, they would only be completing 22 laps, and information passed via pitboards would be effectively two laps old before the driver could react to a developing situation behind him. On a normal three-four mile circuit this would represent, at most, eight miles, but at the Nürburgring it was nearer to 30 miles, and a driver like Fangio can do an awful lot in 30 miles of racing, as he was about to demonstrate.

Race day dawned. It was sunny with a slight breeze to keep the national flags aflutter and thankfully it would stay that way. The grid was drawn up in a 4-3-4 formation. The countdown began with the 'three minutes to go' board. Then, with two minutes remaining, almost simultaneously, 26 engines burst into life, and as if at a signal, mechanics and all scuttled from the grid.

THE RACE IS ON

As the flag fell the two Ferraris rocketed into the lead. Had Fangio's strategy of a lighter car and a quick start come to nought already? It didn't auger well for the rest of the race. Hawthorn and Collins, however, in their efforts to pull away, were in fact slowing one another down by passing and re-passing each other in the early laps. This allowed 'the old man' to keep up with them. By lap three Fangio was in a position to make his move – which he did. First, Collins at Südkehre, then Hawthorn at Adenau. As hard as they tried, the two Ferrari drivers just couldn't hang on to Fangio.

Once past the Ferrari duo, with a clear track in front of him he began to pull away, so that by the end of lap three he led the pair by five seconds, until by lap 11 he had a 28 second lead over them. But, he would need all that, and more, if he was to retain his lead – or at least be in sight of the two Ferraris after the pit stop. These were not novice drivers he was dealing with in second-rate machinery, but top-flight seasoned drivers in state-of-the-art Formula 1 cars.

On lap 12 it was time for Fangio's pit stop. He dived into the pits with his 28 second lead intact. Fangio climbed from the car and proceeded to drink from a water bottle. Calmly and patiently he waited while the mechanics set to work on the car. The seconds ticked inexorably by. The mechanics seemed to be taking an eternity, and their fumbling antics meant that by the time Fangio was on the move again, all his 28 second advantage that he had worked so hard for had evaporated, together with a further 48 seconds. Despite this, during the time in the pits he simply stood calmly, a pool of tranquillity in a sea of frenzied activity, quenching his thirst and no doubt his inner anxiety, but showing no signs of panic whatsoever.

Unbeknown to the Ferrari team and its manager Tavoni, Fangio and the Maserati team manager Giambertone were hatching a plan which was to unfold in the course of the afternoon, whereby Fangio would take it easy during the first two or three laps after the pit stop, then after a signal from Giambertone, Fangio would give it all he could.

The chase was now on, but there were only ten laps of the race left – surely not enough time for Fangio to regain his lead. In the meantime Collins had recorded the fastest lap of the race so far, beating Fangio's fastest lap by 0.6 seconds at 9min 28.9sec.

On lap 14 as Fangio passed the pits (with the gap still at 48 seconds), with a slight nod of Giambertone's head, the plan was put into action. As he did so, black thoughts crossed Giambertone's mind that the plan was too ambitious. Was Fangio up to it now that the

Racing with Heroes

Ferraris lead was so big? Were Hawthorn and Collins sandbagging, did they have a bit in hand? Too late; the die was cast. Giambertone had cried, "Havoc and let slip the dogs of war."

All the cars now had just enough fuel on board to get them through to the end of the race,and were now on an equal footing: Hawthorn and Collins knew this. During those laps following the pit stop the Maserati made no impression on the flying Ferraris in front, in fact Hawthorn had thought that Fangio's car had lost a gear, or that the engine was beginning to misfire. The two Ferrari drivers felt more confident now and were gesturing to one another which one should take the chequered flag (that would never do today, what would Bernie Ecclestone or Max Mosley have said).

After 15 laps the Ferrari's lead over the Maserati was cut by seven seconds. Then, at the end of lap 16 the gap between hunter and hunted was now only 33 seconds.

As the laps went by you could almost hear the clicking of stopwatches from the grandstand, which told their own story. Fangio was catching the leading pair at an unbelievable rate. The crowd and the commentators could hardly believe what they were seeing.

Another lap gone as the two Ferraris slammed past the pits in their desperate effort to try to escape the inevitable. As they did so, Tavoni realised all too late what was happening. They were given the signal at last to go faster – if they could!

Fangio was really going for it now and put in a blistering lap of 9min 28.5sec. He was changing to a higher gear at some corners and taking them faster than he ever had before. He admitted afterwards that he was even frightening himself at some points on the circuit. The technique certainly seemed to be working, and his lap times were tumbling, as he chased the scarlet whirlwind in front of him.

Hawthorn and Collins were almost tripping over one another to go faster, but it was as though they were on a piece of string being pulled backwards into the clutches of the menacing Maserati behind them. Fangio's pit was now telling him that he was closing dramatically on the Ferraris ahead.

Fangio completed lap 18 in 9min 25.3sec, an unbelievable three seconds faster than his previous fastest lap, and had reduced the gap to 20 seconds. Suddenly, there was Collins in front of him as he rounded one of the 275 bends. Of the 22 laps there were now only three, less than 45 miles of racing on this most demanding of all circuits to be completed. The gap was now only13.5 seconds. Surely it was not possible for Fangio to win, but he had other ideas.

The crowds were silent with expectation, looking down the road in the direction of Schwalbenschwanz, trying to be the first to catch a glimpse of the leaders as they hurtled into view.

On lap 20 Fangio had lowered the lap time to an astonishing 9minutes 17.4sec; this performance was running out of superlatives to describe it.

As Fangio reached Südkehre he nipped past Collins, clipping the grass verge, and as he did so, a stone shot from his rear wheel straight into Collins' face and smashed his goggles. Even though he could scarcely see, with the wind tearing at his eyes, Collins retook him on the exit of the corner, only for Fangio to pass him again at Nordkehre and this time make it stick. Collins still chased after the Maserati as best he could in his incapacitated state, but to no avail.

Now they started the penultimate lap. Hawthorn was barely three seconds in front of Fangio: he must have realised that he would inevitably lose his lead, and halfway round the lap, at Aremberg the slow left-hander, it happened. Fangio slipped past on the inside, leaving Hawthorn just enough room. Hawthorn stayed with him and closed in, when suddenly Masten Gregory, who was a lap down, got between them and allowed Fangio to ease away. As they passed the pits to begin their final lap the crowd in the stands erupted, for they had hardly dared to believe what the illuminated sign board had told them earlier.

Hawthorn put his all into that final lap, and in the course of that last 14.17 miles he lost only half a second to the flying Argentinian to follow him over the line only 3.6 seconds adrift. The whole of the crowd were on their feet in tribute, feeling privileged to have seen this unforgettable performance by a quiet man from Argentina and these two young Englishmen.

The three of them stood on the podium. Teacher and pupils; father and sons – Fangio looking slightly relieved, glad it was over. He had just clinched his fifth, and what would be his last, World Championship title. This was to be his last win of a record-breaking career which would last into the next century.

Hawthorn and Collins were full of admiration for this man, a true gentleman on and off the track. They looked just as happy as the winner, for just to have been part of this historic race was reward enough. Fangio for his part was his usual modest self; with the winner's laurel wreath around his neck he put his arms around the two Englishmen in a paternal manner to congratulate them both for a great race, which had been run in the best of spirits, each driver having the greatest of respect for the others.

A crowd of what was estimated to be 100,000 people saw the thrilling spectacle that day, every single one of them staying to the bitter end to witness the outcome of this titanic struggle, which at one stage seemed so one-sided. What an afternoon of racing! The like of which had rarely, if ever, been seen before. This was the victory of a true champion.

Fangio carried on being an excellent ambassador for the sport in later years, but unfortunately both Hawthorn and Collins were to die within the next two. Collins, ironically, was killed during the 1958 German Grand Prix at the Nürburgring (as was Fangio's young protégé Onofre Marimón in 1954). Hawthorn, after having become World Champion at the end of the 1958 season was killed while driving his Jaguar on the Guildford bypass in Surrey, following his retirement from the sport.

This race signalled the pinnacle of Fangio's amazing career and was an example to the young guns on the grid of the difference between a very good driver and a truly great one. No matter how many years in the future great races are chronicled, this race will always be amongst them.

Racing with Heroes

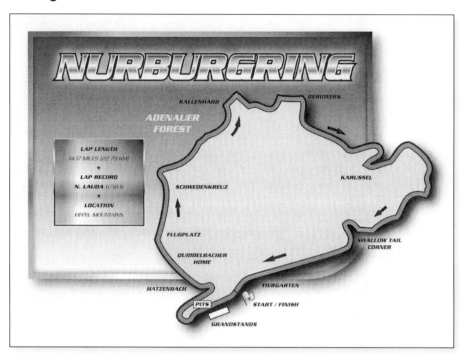

3 MONACO GRAND PRIX - 1961

IN A FAR OFF LAND

ONCE upon a time in a fairy-tale land ruled by a prince and princess by the name of Grimaldi, it was decreed that once a year racing cars would race around the streets of the tiny principality. For three days they would appear, and then, as if by magic, would disappear without trace (well, almost), until the same time the following year. So it had been since 1929 (with a little help from two men by the name of Prince Louis II and Antony Noghès), and so it would continue with their heirs.

The circuit, then, was barely 3.5km in length. The unique setting incorporating – as it still does – the dash through the dimly-lit tunnel before the rush to the chicane and Tabac, then along the yacht-lined harbour to the tight right-hander that was the Gasworks hairpin, past the pits and St Devote. This was then followed by the charge up the hill to Casino Square, past the Casino and the Hotel de Paris into the right-hander Mirabeau, which led onto the frustratingly tight Station hairpin, followed by another right-hander, before plunging once more into the eerie half-light of the tunnel.

For the spectators the sights are dazzling: the boats belonging to celebrities, millionaires and the blue bloods of Europe bobbing on the twinkling blue waters of the harbour, bedecked with scantily-clad sun worshippers, sipping their martinis and Pimms under the Monégasque sun. The palace of Grimaldi and the countless hotels and luxury apartments stacked in tiers in the hillside surrounding the harbour all help to make this a gloriously opulent scene.

Just as Fangio had performed miracles in his last season of racing, so this performance by Moss would enter the annals of motor racing history. This was to be his last full season of Grand Prix racing before his untimely accident at Goodwood during that fateful Easter meeting in 1962, and included arguably two of his most notable wins in Formula 1.

Jack Brabham and Cooper Cars had reigned supreme during 1959 and 1960, but with the change in formula for 1961, which had been posted well in advance of the end of the 1960 season, the tide was about to turn. Earlier on in the year Ferrari had signalled its intentions with the storming success of young Giancarlo Baghetti in Sicily driving the new

60 degree 1.5-litre V6 engined 156. Ferrari had reacted quickly to the change in formula from 2.5-litre to 1.5-litre engine regulations brought in at the end of the 1960 season. By contrast British teams had been slow to react, and had to make do with either last year's Formula 2 engines or hurriedly modified versions of the earlier Coventry Climax engines that were to be designated as Mark 2 versions, neither of which would only very rarely prove to be seriously competitive.

Monaco just happened to be one of those rare occasions in every sense of the word. If the British teams had even the faintest chance of winning anywhere this year, Monaco was the most likely place. It was to be Stirling Moss' third victory at this circuit, a race that all drivers want to win at least once in their career, because of the prestige it carries and the glamour and history of this colourful event.

The final results read as follows; 1st S Moss, 2nd R Ginther, 3rd P Hill, 4th W von Trips, 5th D Gurney, 6th B McLaren. These are the bare facts, but to appreciate this David and Goliath event the whole story must be told. So close and fierce was the racing that day that the fastest lap time of the race was held jointly by Moss and Ginther at 73.2mph.

A CHANGE OF FORMULA

For some inexplicable reason Cooper, Lotus, BRM and the like had not taken the proposed changes to the regulations seriously; now they were to spend the rest of the season trying to recover.

For the 1961 race Ferrari had entered three of their new cars to be driven by Wolfgang "Taffy" von Trips, and the two Californians, Phil Hill and Ritchie Ginther – a formidable team by anyone's reckoning. They were using a mixture of engine types for the type 156, ranging from the 60 degree V6 version to the newer, slightly more powerful 120 degree unit.

The Ferrari team were confident following the practice sessions of the previous two days, which were normally held in the early hours of each morning to minimise disruption to the local population. Moss however had grabbed pole with a lap time of 1min 39.1sec, but Ginther was barely 0.2 seconds slower, and Clark made a supreme effort to take the last place on the front row, but the other two Ferraris hovered ominously in fifth and sixth positions on the grid.

Phil Hill was to line up next to his namesake, Graham, on the grid with a time just 0.2 seconds slower; these two formed the second row. Phil Hill's team-mate von Trips had recorded an almost identical time to put him next to Bruce McLaren, also at 1min 39.8sec, who in turn was within a whisker of the time followed by Tony Brooks in the other BRM. This, then, rounded out the third row.

Of the British teams, Team Lotus and the privateer Rob Walker were in better shape than most, even though Moss would be driving Walker's older Lotus 18 that was some 30-40bhp down on the Ferraris. Jim Clark and Michael May, the Swiss driver, were driving the two Lotuses. The lanky Californian Dan Gurney and the Swedish driver Jo Bonnier were side-by-side on the fourth row with their air-cooled flat-four-cylinder Porsches, the newer flat eight engines were not quite ready yet. A third car for Hans Hermann had also been entered, and, to his credit, he was only fractionally slower; sandwiched in the middle of the fifth row by Surtees and May.

Jack Brabham and Bruce McLaren were again driving Coventry Climax-engined Coopers for the 1961 season. In fact, all the British teams were running an interim or modified version of the previous year's Formula 2 Climax engine while they awaited the new V8, which wouldn't arrive until much later in the season (for the German Grand Prix), and then only in limited numbers. Things didn't look too good in the English camps.

The main objective when driving at Monaco is to drive in a smooth and tidy fashion. It was always easy to identify the ones that didn't by the amount of whitewash on the walls of their tyres as they brushed against the newly painted kerbs. Suspension and steering parts do not take too kindly to this type of abuse and will either break instantly or, worse still, later on around the circuit when the driver least expects it. Overtaking on a circuit like this is never easy, so it is important to qualify well and be as far up the grid as you can be, and try to keep out of every one else's way, particularly at the start.

Practice had been a strange affair, for it had been decided by 'the powers that be' to only allow 16 cars of the 21 that had entered to race. 12 guaranteed places had been allocated, which left nine drivers scrapping for the four remaining places on the grid.

Unfortunately, drivers such as Innes Ireland, who had trouble during practice, did not get into the race. In fact, Ireland's problem was no trivial affair. During one of his qualifying runs he was caught-out by the revised gate pattern of the new Lotus and selected the wrong gear in the ZF 'box while entering the tunnel. This resulted in the rear wheels locking up, throwing the car into the tunnel wall and throwing Innes out of the car in the process. Luckily he suffered no more than cuts and bruises and a bang to his knee. Clark, in the meantime, had mixed fortunes, for, after setting the first sub 1min 40sec lap, he crashed into one of the guard rails introduced around the circuit and badly damaged the car. There was much doubt as to whether the care would be ready in time for the race. Race mechanics can perform miracles, however, and often do. By dint of much burning of the mythical midnight oil, the car was ready just in time.

With Innes and his car out of the race, an extra slot became available, and, in the end, the five lucky drivers were Ritchie Ginther, John Surtees, Hans Hermann, Michael May, and the Englishman Cliff Allison. Jack Brabham had previously committed himself to racing at Indianapolis and had to fly out to qualify for this immediately after the first practice session, during which he set a time of 1min 44sec. Unfortunately this time left him at the back of the grid for the race, for which he barely arrived in time.

It was during the second practice session that Ginther proved his worth, with a time of 1min 39.25sec, pipping Clark's time of 1min 39.61sec, which was equalled by Graham Hill in his BRM. Hill was to become one of the masters of Monaco in the years to come, greeting the Prince for the winner's prize on an almost regular basis. Though some might argue that he did not have the natural talent of Fangio, Clark or Senna, there are not many drivers who can lay claim to having won the Formula 1 World Champion's crown

Racing with Heroes

on two occasions, won at Monte Carlo on no less than five occasions, as well as having won at Le Mans and the Indianapolis 500 (representing the triple crown of motor racing). His unfortunate death in 1975 certainly cheated the racing world of a great driver and personality, the like of which is sorely missed in this day and age.

The tail end of the grid was then made up of Michael May, Hans Hermann, John Surtees, Maurice Trintignant, Cliff Allison, and the jet-lagged Jack Brabham, in that order.

The start of the race was even more precarious in those days because the start line was just a short dash from the 180 degree corner known as the Gasworks Hairpin (now Rascasse). There was usually some poor unfortunate or two, who was elbowed off line, or came to grief at this first corner even though it was usually taken at no more than 40mph.

This time however, after the veteran French driver Louis Chiron dropped the flag, they all got away to an unbelievably orderly start. As they rounded the first corner it was the scarlet Ferrari of Ginther that got the drop on the others and set off like a greyhound from the traps, with Clark struggling to keep up, such was Ginther's pace.

Moss followed Clark with Gurney, Brooks, Bonnier and Phil Hill in close attendance as they charged up the hill from St Devote to the Casino. Across the square they chased like a pack of hounds snapping at one another's heels (or should that be wheels). Surely they couldn't keep this up for another giddying 99 laps. Surely the machinery could not keep this up for another 99 laps!

The fact that the laps are short, the kerbs and the guardrails seem to get ever-closer each lap, the contrast of the bright spring sunshine before entering the dimly lit tunnel then back out into the vivid daylight again, all adds up to the fact that laps are pretty frenetic. Lap speeds may be relatively low, but with each corner following so quickly upon another there is no time to rest on this circuit (although Moss always seemed to have time to pick out a pretty girl in the crowd and wave to her each lap).

Clark was having trouble keeping up with Ginther, and it wasn't long before he was in the pits, the Lotus suffering from fuel pump problems. So it was left to Moss to whittle away at Ginther's lead. Slowly and relentlessly he hauled Ginther in, while at the same time dragging Bonnier along with him. These two had now opened up a bit of a gap on the remainder of the field, and by lap 11 had closed up onto the menacing tail pipes of the Ferrari: three laps later they were both past.

While all this was going on, first Phil Hill and then von Trips squeezed past Brooks and Gurney, thus forming up in line astern of their team-mate Ginther; now they could act in unison. This left Gurney and Brooks at the back of the pack trying to keep up with Surtees and McLaren, who were hotly disputing sixth place. McLaren would in fact finish the race in sixth, albeit five laps down on the winner.

By lap 17 Graham Hill's BRM had succumbed to a seized fuel pump. The Ferrari three-pronged attack now gathered momentum, and although by lap 22 Ginther had noticeably dropped off the back of the leading pair, Hill was impatient to get past his team-mate, and in another two laps had done so and set off after the leaders. Shortly after this von Trips also got ahead of Ginther.

Monaco is a notoriously difficult circuit at which to overtake unless the driver is ready to be overtaken, and neither Bonnier or Moss were going to make it easy for their pursuers. Now the pressure was on Bonnier, for Hill was breathing down his neck. Then, in a daring dive down the inside, Hill moved ahead of Bonnier. Unfortunately, the latter's backward slide didn't stop there, for behind Bonnier, Ginther was regrouping and re-passed von Trips for fourth place.

By lap 41 Ginther was back in his stride once more and got past Bonnier. Although the Ferrari were clearly faster, Moss seemed to make up for it through the tight turns and twisty sections, of which Monaco has no shortage. With the side panels removed to keep him cool, Moss threaded the Lotus through the narrow streets of the principality with all the dexterity and slight of hand of an illusionist performing tricks that he had done a thousand times before, mystifying not only the spectators but the other drivers in the process. For lap after lap, round and round the circuit he guided the little blue car as though on rails, picking off the back markers as he lapped them with unabated speed.

After 42 laps Moss held a ten second lead over Hill and Ginther, with von Trips eager to get past Bonnier. But even for Moss it was difficult to maintain the gap, and slowly – tenth of a second-by-tenth of a second – the two Ferraris began to close the gap, and Ginther was now pushing Hill. By lap 60 Bonnier was still game, but his car had given up the ghost and his engine expired. The Swede had done as much as he could on this historic afternoon, but his luck was out. This meant, however, that the entire Ferrari team were now in line astern of the Rob Walker Lotus and closing. Still the white-helmeted Moss managed to hang on.

Von Trips now started to fall back, his car experiencing some kind of electrical malaise. Meanwhile, Brooks also had engine problems with his BRM, and had to call it a day, thus promoting Surtees to fifth spot. This order only lasted until lap 69, when Surtees in the Yeoman Credit Cooper ground to a halt at the Station Hairpin, allowing McLaren in the works Cooper into fifth position.

Meanwhile, back at the front, the scarlet train continued to push and harry Moss for the lead, but still to no avail; still the Rob Walker-entered Lotus nimbly carried on picking its way through the backmarkers. The Ferraris were now really putting Moss under pressure and, as they approached the last quarter of the race, the gap began to come down, lap-by-lap, as they chipped away at his lead. By lap 85 the gap was down to 3.1 seconds, despite the fact that Moss had just set equal fastest lap of the race in his response to Ginther's with an identical time on the previous lap. With 15 laps still to go Moss just had to hold on, keep to the racing line, and concentrate on keeping the car away from the walls, the barriers, and the kerbs.

It was Ginther who was now taking the race to Moss in the last phase as Hill began to fall back, and so it was now a straight fight between the two. With only five laps to go Moss had managed to extend his lead to five seconds, but Ginther had still not given up, and started to come back at Moss once again. It was not to be, however, and, as Moss crossed the line to take the chequered flag, Ginther was to follow some 3.6 seconds later.

Racing with Heroes

Moss' first win at Monte Carlo was in 1956 at the wheel of a Maserati 250F; his next win at the principality wasn't until 1960 when he drove the Rob Walker Lotus 18. This then was his third win, and none more deserved, having defeated the entire Ferrari team single-handed with a car that was approximately 15 per cent down on power to the might of Maranello.

Little did the Italian team realise that although they may resoundingly defeat the other teams for the rest of the season, Moss would again thwart their efforts at the most challenging of all circuits, the Nürburgring in Germany later in the year. But that is another story for another day.

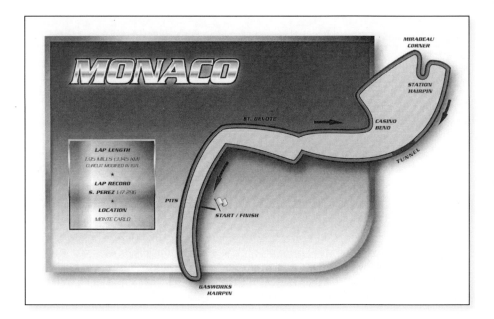

4 LE MANS – 1969

A RACE OF ENDURANCE

OVER the years Le Mans has seen some epic races, some torrential weather, some tragic disasters, and some stories of human strength and courage that require a book all of their own. This particular chapter captures just one episode in this epic event's history.

The first vingt quatre heures du Mans was run on the closed roads around the town of Le Mans in 1923. This followed a number of fatal accidents in earlier city-to-city races, notably the Paris–Madrid race of 1903, where eight people were killed. As a result, it was felt that racing should be contained within purpose-made tracks for such events.

The 24 hours endurance race at the Sarthe circuit is unique. It has, from time-to-time, had changes made to its regulations and format, as well as the circuit itself, but it still remains the same technical and physical challenge it always was. Since the inaugural race which took place 26-27 May 1923, and was won by André Lagache and René Léonard in a Chenard and Walcker Sport, some great names have left their mark in the record books. Names such as, Raymond Sommer, Pierre Levegh, Jacky Ickx, Derek Bell, Tom Kristensen, Olivier Gendebien, and not least The Bentley Boys, from 1927-1930. As well as the drivers, great marques such as Maserati, Ferrari, Porsche, Jaguar, Ford, Audi, Bentley, not forgetting Aston Martin, have also carved their names with pride on this piece of French countryside. There was a ten year break during the war years, from 1939 to 1949, but to this day the race continues to be a main attraction in the racing calendar. Unfortunately, other similar high profile races of nine, 12, and 24 hour duration at circuits such as Reims and Spa Francorchamp have now ceased to exist for one reason or another.

It offers a completely different challenge to the two-three hour sprint that a Grand Prix represents. It is a gruelling test of endurance for cars and drivers alike, and it has to be approached by the entrants in a more planned, tactical manner – involving months of meticulous planning and preparation.

Many of the top Grand Prix drivers consider this race too dangerous and will not compete. Although to be fair, in the current climate of contracts and sponsorship deals, they are prevented from taking part even if they wanted to. The fact that there can be a

Racing with Heroes

difference of 100mph or more between the top speeds of the faster cars (travelling at up to 240mph), and the slower cars, makes overtaking very hazardous, especially at night with rain lashing the circuit, as it has been known to on many occasions. Even worse is the mist and fog that can appear during the cold half-light in the early hours of dawn. Tiredness is also a key factor during those early hours of Sunday morning, 12 or 14 hours into the race. Add to this the fact that some of the drivers of lesser teams will not have the experience required to keep them out of harm's way, and it becomes a very dangerous mix. Maybe those drivers that opt out are right – there have been a number of fatalities over the years; the most notable being the disaster of 1955, when nearly 80 spectators were killed after the Mercedes of Pierre Levegh flew into the packed main grandstand at high speed, after being launched into the air following his collision with the Austin Healey of Lance Macklin. Lance was lucky to escape with his life, but not so poor Pierre Levegh, who had been rewarded for his gutsy drive two years earlier by being invited by Mercedes-Benz to drive for it in this fateful race. But people like Ickx, Bell, Moss, Hawthorn and Fangio relished the challenge, and proved themselves to be true gladiators of the circuits.

The event is not just a race; it is more of a carnival weekend, with a motor race going on at the same time. The atmosphere is unique and attracts spectators from around the world. Although in recent years it seems to have lost some of its prestige and glamour, it still remains a very significant race on the motorsport calendar. Many anecdotes have been told over the years about the race, such as the one about the over-zealous driver who sprinted across the track, following the drop of the tricolour to start the race, but instead of leaping into the car, vaulted clear over it to land in a heap on the ground beside it. Or of the driver who on reaching his car climbed in, only to put his foot through the steering wheel, and spent the next few seconds trying to extricate himself as half the field roared off into the distance. Or of the competitor who replenished his overheating radiator by answering a call of nature. Alas, the spectacle of the drivers lined up on one side of the track before sprinting to their cars, arranged in echelon on the other side, has now been dropped (in the pursuit of greater safety) in favour of a rolling start, which is unquestionably safer, but not nearly so exciting for the spectator.

The 24-hour endurance is a popular race with British enthusiasts, thousands of whom make the pilgrimage each year by air, road, rail and sea. Some will endure an 18-hour coach journey just to get there. Many take their tents to camp out over the long weekend, eating and drinking al fresco to the accompaniment of the raucous sounds emanating from the track nearby, which no doubt is music to their ears.

For 1969, the main contest would be the fight between the Ford GT40s and the Porsche 917s, backed up by the 908s. Ford had wanted to get a foothold in this form of racing for some time, but for one reason or another its plans had been thwarted, until, that is, it came across the Eric Broadley-designed Lola, which became the basis of the GT40, standing as it did barely 40 inches off the ground. And so a legend was born.

Of the cars entered in the larger-engined category there were seven Porsches, five Ford GT40s, four Ferraris, four Matras, and four Renault Gordinis. Before the race had even started Porsche ran into problems at the pre-race scrutineering session regarding the moveable parts of its rear aerofoils. The officials wanted these removed, claiming that they contravened the current FIA regulations. Porsche was not happy to do this, arguing that they were an integral part of the aerofoil design and that without them the cars would be unstable and dangerous to drive. In the end the officials relented, following Porsche's threat to withdraw its cars, and the aerofoil stayed intact.

Due to the presidential elections that were taking place that weekend, instead of the race starting at its usual time of four o'clock on the Saturday afternoon, it had been brought forward to two o'clock. The second hand of the Dutray clock over the pits ticked the seconds metronomically away until, on the stroke of two, the tricolour dropped, and 45 drivers ran across the track to their cars. Sorry; make that 44 drivers. A certain Belgian chappie by the name of Jacky Ickx, who, to underline his protest that the current starting pattern was too dangerous and was an almighty accident waiting to happen, did not run. He walked calmly across to his car, got in, buckled up his belts, started the engine and drove away at the tail of the field. Would he live to regret this decision? Only the next 24 hours would tell.

In a flurry of action, the high-speed traffic jam was under way. It was the Porsche 917 – #14 driven by Rolf Stommelen – that led at the start of the first lap, closely followed by Jo Siffert's Porsche 908 #33 (to be co-driven by Brian Redman), Vic Elford in Porsche 917 #12, and Schutz in the Porsche 908 #46. As they flashed past the pits and under the Dunlop bridge with the leaders still in a tight bunch, the smaller classes were already beginning to lose contact. This was the first lap of many to be covered before 2pm tomorrow, but not all would last the distance. As they swept under the Dunlop bridge once more to complete their first lap, Elford was up to second.

Less than an hour had elapsed before the ominous sign of black smoke could be seen rising skywards near Whitehouse: later to be confirmed as the wreckage of John Woolf's privately entered Porsche 917, which had fatally crashed and burst into flames on lap four. Unfortunately, a river of burning petrol had spread across the track and Amon's car had to be extinguished after it caught alight after driving through the flaming fuel. This prompted the organisers to consider restarting the race, but the idea was dismissed and the race continued.

After just over an hour, Siffert in the Spyder (car #20), moved into the lead following the first round of pit stops, with Stommelen dropping back with an oil leak, although at this point Porsche filled the first five places.

By a quarter to five the Ickx/Oliver mark IV GT40 was already up into 14th spot and looking good. By 6pm it was up to seventh, but would those precious few seconds that Ickx sacrificed at the start prove critical later in the race? It was also about this time that Siffert's race had come to an end after his car succumbed to gearbox problems.

As the evening wore on and daylight gave way to dusk, and the attractions of the fairground and stalls became more intrusive, the Elford/Attwood car took over the lead and, just after 9pm, the John Wyer Ford GT40 of Ickx and Oliver was in a menacing 5th place.

Racing with Heroes

Now the skies darkened and the cars swished by with headlamps ablaze, we were now entering the dangerous period of the race, for even in the gathering gloom the cars, like the leading Porsche, were still hammering down the Mulsanne straight at undiminished speeds of around 240mph.

After midnight the Stommelen/Ahrens 917 was brought into the pits in an effort to stem the flow of leaking oil that had been getting worse lap after lap. The car was to spend two hours in the pits before finally being pushed into the "dead car park" which was already beginning to fill. While the drivers were working harder than ever to push on through the darkness the spectators began to drift away, either to visit the fairground and stalls, to feed the inner man, to top up their alcohol level, or simply to get some long-awaited shuteye. The hardened enthusiasts sat huddled in the gloom, endeavouring to keep track of the night's events at the same time as keeping warm.

For hour after hour the headlights of the cars cut tramlines of light through the darkness, lasting a second or two until car and driver once again disappear into the dark cloak of night.

In the pits, in spite of the darkness, the weather, and the fatigue, everything must carry on as usual. With monotonous regularity mechanics change the tyres, refuel the cars, clean the windscreens, change the brake pads, listen to the drivers moans and groans about the car and send the replacement driver quickly on his way again, and if everything is running normally, repeat the process in an hours time – or thereabouts. If things are not running to plan they may have to replace a clutch or a gearbox, or make bodywork repairs, or resolve an electrical malfunction, or plug an oil leak before sending the car out into the night once more. An endurance race is tough on the cars, but is as equally unrelenting for the drivers, the mechanics – in fact everyone concerned with getting the car through those wearying 24 hours.

As dawn started to break in the east, so the travel-stained cars appeared from the shrouding early morning mist, but there were fewer of them now; the long hours of darkness had taken their toll on both men and machinery. After the ravages of the night it was Elford in the lead, followed by Lins, with Oliver in third place. At this stage there was no clue as to how close the finish would be come two o' clock. Some of the remaining cars were now limping around the circuit (hobbled by a mechanical or electrical problem), in the hope that they could make it to the finish without a lengthy delay for repairs which may be fruitless anyway. If the cars looked somewhat the worse-for-wear, the same could also be said for the drivers, having made it through with little or no sleep. It is hardly surprising that more errors are made during these early hours of Sunday morning than at any other time during the weekend: the drivers know there is still another eight hours or more to go before they can relax. As the morning wore on, it now looked like a straight fight between the Porsche 908 #64 of Hans Hermann and Gerard Larrousse and the Ford GT40 #6 driven by Jacky Ickx and Jackie Oliver ... if both cars lasted the distance, that is. The Porsche had proved to be fast – there was no doubting that – but they seemed a little fragile; the Ford however, looked strong. The Elford/Attwood 917 had retired just before 11 o' clock, sans clutch. Over the course of the final two hours, the race developed into a sprint to the finish, with the lead changing at the pit stops as well as on the track. In the closing stages the cars were trading places three or four times a lap as the drivers tried to shrug off the languor of the previous 22 hours efforts. They summoned all their physical and mental strength and concentration for one last sustained push to the finish. Who would be the stronger come two o' clock? Hailwood, in the other GT40, tried to help by getting between the Ford and the Porsche, but could not maintain this for long. The number 7 car did, however, hang-on to make it over the line in third place at the finish. With nearly 24 hours gone, Le Mans had never seen such a close, hard-fought finish. With no quarter being given on either side, into the last lap they went, fighting tooth and nail. Just before the drop of the flag at 2pm to signal the end of the race, both cars blasted across the line less than a second apart. This meant that they would have to complete another lap before the winner could be declared. As one, the spectators that packed the stands and enclosures craned their necks to see who would emerge first from Whitehouse onto the finishing straight. It was the blue and orange colours of the John Wyer entered GT40 that flashed into view, Ickx was at the wheel, leading the Porsche driven by Herman by a matter of yards, to take the honours at the end of an epic 24 hours. As the two cars crossed the line just over 24 hours after the drop of the flag the day before, there was barely 100 yards between them. The two Jackies had done a superb job in bringing the mark IV Ford GT40 home in first position to realise Ford's dreams of winning the Le Mans 24 hour race of endurance. But a thought must be spared for Hans Hermann and Gerard Larrousse in the second placed Porsche 908, having battled so hard right up to the last. Only 14 cars were to finish the race with 31 falling by the wayside for one reason or another. It truly was a race of endurance. This was to be the first of six wins at Le Mans for Jacky Ickx, three of them with Derek Bell, who went on to become a five times winner himself. The final classified result sheet read as follows:

1st Jacky Ickx/Jackie Oliver Ford GT40 No 6; 2nd Hans Hermann/Gerard Larrousse Porsche 908 No 64; 3rd David Hobbs/Mike Hailwood Ford GT40 car No 7; 4th Jean-Pierre Beltoise/Piers Courage Matra MS 650 Spyder No 33; 5th Jean Guichet/Nino Vaccarella Matra MS 630 Coupe No 32; 6th John Wyer entered. Helmut Kelleners/Reinhold Joest car No 68.

These are the top six of the 14 classified finishers of the race from 45 starters. The fastest lap of the race was recorded by Vic Elford at an average speed of 234.02kph, a time of 3min 27.2sec in the 917.

Racing with Heroes

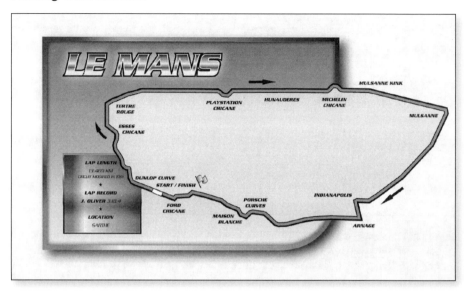

5 BRAZILIAN GRAND PRIX – 2008

IT'S NOT OVER 'TIL IT'S OVER

THE champagne that had been showered over everyone and everything within spraying distance moments before would soon become a sticky morass on the podium. Even so, the team managers, CEOs and designers were already focusing their thoughts on the forthcoming season and next year's cars, which were, even now, past the drawing board stage.

In 2007 Lewis Hamilton was the upstart rookie who sought to depose the 2006 world Champion, Fernando Alonso, of his crown in his very first year in Formula 1. He very nearly made it too – but in this, his record-breaking year, he ruffled a few feathers along the way. He also made a number of elementary mistakes. Some would say he tried to run before he could walk, some that he should have spent that first year learning from his teammate Alonso, as Moss had done with Fangio and others before him. Today, Formula 1 isn't the unforgiving sport it used to be, where a driver simply couldn't afford to learn by his mistakes, as they too often proved fatal.

Undoubtedly, Hamilton has a talent that from day one he wanted to show the world. In 2007 he was driving for the very successful McLaren team, whose CEO Ron Dennis had nurtured and encouraged this formidable talent from an early age. For his Formula 1 debut season Hamilton was teamed up with the 2005-2006 World Champion Fernando Alonso, who is an equally talented and determined young man. Throughout the season there had been clashes of opinion and temperament (not to mention wheels) between the two drivers. They seemed to grow further apart as race followed race and they criss-crossed the world weekend after weekend, trying to prove who was the better of the two.

For the 2008 season Alonso left McLaren to return to Renault, the team with which he had won his two World Championships. He had become disenchanted by the treatment he had received at McLaren, believing that he would never get a fair deal as part of the British team while there was a British driver. Unfortunately for Alonso, 2008 was not to be a good year for Renault, whose R28 did not start to perform at its best until two thirds of the way through the season, when he had lost all chance of challenging for the title. As the season drew towards its end, there were to be only three serious contenders: Räikkonën,

37

Racing with Heroes

the current World Champion, in his Ferrari, Felipe Massa also driving for Ferrari, and Lewis Hamilton, still with the McLaren team. With only one race to go, Hamilton was in a good position to clinch the title, with a seven point lead over Massa, and with 25 points on Räikkonën, now out of contention.

Hamilton was still learning his trade, but did not appear to take on board advice given to him by older and wiser heads, who had been in the sport a lot longer than he. After having made a good start to the season he, made some errors of judgement, and consequently the championship went down to the wire in Brazil when it should have been wrapped up in his favour long before.

The current Sao Paulo circuit, home of the Brazilian Grand Prix in recent years, is 2.67 miles long (reduced from its original 4.95 miles), and is located in its southern suburbs. It is known as the Interlagos circuit as well as The Autódromo José Carlos Pace. For 2008 it was to host the final grand épreuve of the season, just as it had done the previous year. And, as in the previous year, it was to decide the year long tussle between drivers from the Ferrari and McLaren teams for the World Championship. In 2007 it was between Kimi Räikkonën, Fernando Alonso and Lewis Hamilton; Räikkonën taking it by one point.

THE WEATHER INTERVENES

The cars were lined up on the grid with the track temperature at nearly 40 degrees centigrade, but five minutes before the scheduled start time of the race, the famously unpredictable Interlagos rain started to fall. It was more than just a sprinkling, it was enough to delay the start for a change to wet tyres as the track ran wet (as did Bernie Ecclestone after getting caught in his shirt sleeves in the downpour) in some parts, but remained dry in others.

With the tension already heightened by the fact that this was the deciding race of the season, the delay didn't help the taut nerves of the drivers and teams. This was only the start of what was to prove a race of changing fortunes, right up to the very last controversial corner.

Controversy was something that McLaren, Ron Dennis and Lewis Hamilton had battled with over the past two seasons, from being accused of technical espionage, to media headlines of the two drivers (Alonso and Hamilton) almost coming to blows with one another in 2007. Hamilton had also upset a number of other drivers earlier on in the 2008 season at Monza, with his driving attitude on the track, which was felt to be unnecessarily aggressive, bordering on dangerous.

Practice could have gone better for Hamilton, but his fourth place on the grid was not a disaster. His intention was simply to drive a steady race (so he said), stay out of trouble and to finish within the top five, for even if Massa won, Hamilton would still have enough points to take the championship.

Pole had been snatched by Massa from the one lap master, Jarno Trulli, who really pulled out all the stops in his Toyota and slotted himself between the two Ferraris as Räikkonën pipped Hamilton, while his teammate Kovalainen was close behind in fifth spot. Alonso, the ever-present threat, could only make it into sixth on the grid. These drivers filled the first three rows, with the likes of the two Red Bull-sponsored teams and Toyota hovering in the background, ready to spoil someone's day.

Now the grid was a frenzy of mechanics changing wheels as the cars stood on the grid. But the burning question was how long would the rain last? Would it be a case of the cars having to return to the pits within a few laps for dry weather tyres again? This would obviously upset the game plan for those who had chosen to run with a heavy fuel load for the minimum number of stops. Or, would it continue and increase in intensity, as had been seen at this track in the past, making conditions undriveable?

It was expected in the race that Räikkonën would play a supporting role to Massa, but what would Kovalainen be able to do to help Hamilton?

When the lights turned from red to green to signal the start of the race it was initially an orderly start until Coulthard, in the last Formula 1 race of his career, was tagged by Nakajima going into turn one, and ignominiously finished his race there and then in the 'kitty litter' of the run-off area.

Massa had made a good clean start, with Hamilton slotting into fourth place behind Trulli in second and Räikkonën in third. At the end of the first lap these front four were followed across the line by Vettel, Alonso, Kovalainen, Bourdais, Glock, Webber, Barrichello, Kubica, Sutil, Button, Rosberg and Fisichella.

Following his coming together with David Coulthard, Nakajima came into the pits. Nelson Piquet Jr also failed to make it round to complete his first lap after spinning off, damaging the car, and bringing out the safety car for three laps. During this time 'Fisi' was called in to change to dry tyres, as the track now appeared to be drying out quite quickly – a move that was to give him good 'track position' for a while.

At this point Alonso was in sixth place, which could have been a threat to Hamilton. Kovalainen was to support Hamilton by keeping Alonso behind him, so on lap five, Kovalainen tried to outbrake Alonso going in to the Esses. He did this successfully, but went wide on the exit, allowing Alonso back in front.

By the end of lap seven the rest of the field followed Fisi's example and started to come in for dry tyres, as the track now had a definite dry line almost everywhere. Rosberg and Button were the first, followed by the rest a lap or two later. Massa and Hamilton were, in fact, the last two to come in – Massa on lap ten, Hamilton on lap eleven.

After the round of pit stops it was Vettel who was now pushing Massa. He had changed tyres earlier, and so maximised his advantage, also being on a lighter fuel load. Somehow though, one got the feeling that Massa was driving within his capabilities and appeared to be the master of the situation. All was perfectly controlled; he was driving a great race and dictating the pace at which he wanted to drive.

Hamilton meanwhile was now in seventh following his late stop, with Trulli in sixth and Alonso having jumped to claim third spot in the Renault. Here was another driver driving a beautifully controlled race.

Fisichella now found himself fifth following his early stop but under pressure from the other drivers, despite being just over a second off the pace of the leading cars. He must have known he wouldn't be able to hold this position for long, but he was going to make the most of it in the meantime.

On lap 12 Hamilton hustled his way past Trulli but only just managed it; as he exited the turn he slid wildly with a handful of opposite lock, but still managed to make it stick. Unfortunately for Trulli, he had a similar moment shortly afterwards, but failed to control it. In the ensuing moments teammate Glock and Sebastian Bourdais flashed past him.

The Esses is a favourite place to pass at this track, and on lap 18 Lewis used it to pass Fisichella. This now took him up to that vital fifth place that he so badly needed for the championship but all was not safe just yet, as Glock now loomed large in Hamilton's mirrors forcing him to fight for the position.

There were almost two separate races going on; one with drivers who wanted to drive fast enough to hold station and keep safely out of harms way, while there were others who had nothing to lose and simply wanted a good result at the end of a long hard season.

Fisichella was now seriously holding Bourdais and Trulli up, until lap 21 when Trulli tried to outbrake him, where else, but at the Esses. It nearly ended in tears as Bourdais ended up taking the escape road to avoid a coming together with the other two. Jarno didn't quite make it past Fisi whose surprising straight line speed managed to keep Trulli behind him, for now.

By the 23rd lap Massa and Vettel were pretty evenly matched at the front, but Massa was looking comfortable as he controlling the pace, and on lap 27 Vettel made his second pit stop of the race, thus giving Massa a bit of breathing space. This was completely out of sync with the others, and was obviously a tactical move.

Alonso in the meantime had dropped off the back of the leading duo, as had Räikkonën who was now a distant fourth, staying ahead of Hamilton and the chasing Timo Glock. Following his pit stop Vettel now rejoined in sixth spot behind Hamilton and Glock. Glock was to make his second pit stop on lap 36, which was to drop him to fourteenth position, thus relieving the worry McLaren had that Glock may demote Hamilton to below fifth place and out of his title-winning position: a worry that Ron Dennis tried to overcome by urging Kovalainen to up his pace, which he did by passing Trulli and Fisichella. This saw Kovalainen in fifth place on lap 40. Meanwhile on lap 39 following Massa's pit stop, Alonso popped up in the lead but this lasted for just one lap until he too pitted (along with Hamilton), letting Räikkonën take his turn in front for two laps, after which Massa resumed his rightful place at the head of the field. The little Brazilian was really putting in a mature performance; not getting carried away at all by the occasion, which could easily have been his undoing, especially on his home soil.

Almost when it seemed things had settled down after the second round of pit stops, news came that more rain was expected for the last few minutes of the race. Would it come? Would it be heavy? Would the drivers be able to see out those last few minutes on the dry tyres they were currently on? All that could be done was wait and see.

Lap 45 saw Massa leading Vettel once more, followed by Alonso, Räikkonën,

Hamilton and Kovalainen in the top six places. Unfortunately, Vettel needed a further pit stop around lap 51, which was bound to drop him out of the top three, but with the aforementioned threat of rain, who could tell how things would now work out? Things were getting tense for Hamilton, but luck, it seemed, was on his side. For as Vettel left the pits after what was meant to be his final stop, he came out just behind Hamilton, elevating the McLaren driver to fourth place – one place better than he needed. But, with his fresh tyres Vettel was making things very uncomfortable for the young Englishman. Likewise Räikkonën was beginning to pressurise Alonso after putting in some very good lap times.

As the remaining laps ran out so the skies began to cloud over just as predicted, with timing that was to bring this last race of the season to a dramatic end, one that Harold Pinter in his heyday could not have bettered. Sure enough, with just six laps to go, it began to rain again, lightly at first. It was Fisi who blinked first, gambling on a change to extreme wets in an attempt to make up for his earlier pit stop, when a problem with his clutch delayed him. At this stage he had nothing to lose and possibly much to gain.

By lap 66, both Räikkonën and Kovalainen had come in for wets too, in an attempt to improve their lap times, for although it was beginning to rain more heavily now, it was still quite patchy on the circuit.

The point was made; the stopwatches and the weather decided the matter; and on lap 67 Hamilton and Massa both came in for wets, together with a number of other drivers. At the end of the pit stops Massa was once more back in the lead followed by Alonso, Räikkonën, Glock, Hamilton and Vettel. Glock however hadn't come in for wets, and was still hoping to make it home on his ageing set of dry tyres. At this stage he was putting in faster lap times than Massa. What a finish this was going to be!

With two laps left the rain increased in strength and it was all beginning to kick off. Vettel passed Hamilton as they went through Junção, demoting him to sixth place. This was not in the McLaren game plan, and they urged him over the radio to retake Vettel. After his first lap on wets Massa returned a lap time of 1min 19.8sec, while Glock, still on his set of dry tyres, clocked 1min 18.7sec. Still the rain came.

The championship looked as though it was heading Massa's way; there was now only one lap to go. Still the rain came.

Massa, Alonso and Räikkonën all held station up front but on this, the last lap, things were about to happen. Glock's previous lap time was slower but not sufficiently so to cause alarm. However, on the last lap the car was becoming more difficult to control, and he suddenly started to lose ground. In the meantime Massa had crossed the finishing line and had been told he was the new World Champion – he punched the air as he crossed the line, and his pit crew and family all hugged one another with jubilation.

Unfortunately their joy was short-lived, for out on the circuit as they approached the last Corner, Glock was struggling to keep his car on the road. He ran wide, even at reduced speed and as he did so, Hamilton made a lunge and was past in an instant to get those all important points for fifth place, which would see him crowned as the new Formula 1 World Champion for 2008.

Racing with Heroes

The cheers and the hugs and the congratulations switched in a matter of seconds from Massa's pit to that of Hamilton, and Massa's tears of joy turned to tears of bitter disappointment. Such are the fortunes of motor racing, where nothing can be taken for granted, even after the chequered flag has fallen. Revenge is sweet, and Hamilton had turned the tables by pipping Massa by one championship point to the title, just as Räikkönen and Ferrari had beaten him the previous season.

And so the 2008 season reached its nail-biting climax, with smiles for some teams, tears for others, and perhaps relief and disappointment for the rest. Ah well, there's always next year! Little did they know then what the winter months and the new season would bring, for a new team was about to appear on the scene that would surprise them all.

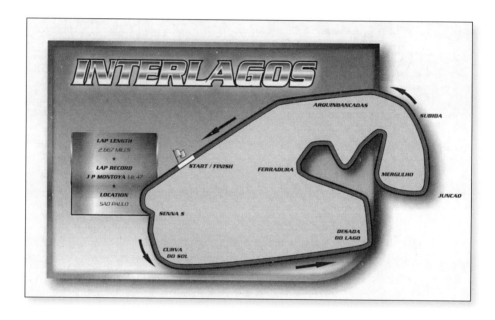

6 FRENCH GRAND PRIX – 1959

TOAST OF THE CHAMPAGNE REGION

THE Reims circuit today is but a shadow of its former glory. The years have not been kind to this once splendid arena. Time, weather, and neglect have ravaged this previously revered race track, which has seen some of the greatest drivers exhibit their gladiatorial skills. Even so, I am sure at certain times of the year the ghosts of those great men and their racing machines can be seen thundering around the circuit; the stands vibrating with the roar of their engines and the cheering of the spectators, before silence is restored, and it once again becomes just an empty hulk, with the wind and the dust blowing through it, with just a hint of exhaust fumes and hot engine oil hanging in the spirited air. Sic transit gloria mundi.

The 45th French Grand Prix of 1959 was to be a race of attrition for the drivers as well as the cars. It was run in extremely hot conditions which became more intolerable as the race wore on. Since midway through the previous week, when practice had taken place, the weather had been dry and warm in the Champagne region. As race day dawned with a cloudless blue sky, the temperature built, until by 2pm when the race started, it was scorching, and the metal of the cars and the tarmac of the roads became unbearable to the touch. Practice had been a sobering affair for the English teams of Lotus Cooper and BRM, for Reims was a high speed power circuit where driver ability was countered by sheer horsepower. Claims by Ferrari earlier on in the season of their V6 engines giving 295bhp were considered by some cynics to be optimistic, but these doubters were to be silenced in France.

Ferrari had five cars present to be driven by Jean Behra, Tony Brooks, Phil Hill, Dan Gurney and Olivier Gendebien, while Cooper had three cars for Jack Brabham, Bruce McLaren and Masten Gregory, the bespectacled American. BRM arrived with cars for the Swede Jo Bonnier, Harry Schell, and Ron Flockhart. Stirling Moss would be driving the British Racing Partnership entered BRM – the same one in fact that he would be using for the British Grand Prix at Aintree in just under two weeks time. Maurice Trintignant was entered with the Rob Walker Cooper Climax. The remainder of the field was made up of three Cooper Maseratis for Roy Salvadori, Ian Burgess and Colin Davis, and three ageing

Racing with Heroes

Maserati 250Fs to be driven by De Beaufort, Scarlatti and d'Orey, the South American driver. This then was the field of 21 cars (it should have been 22, but Bayardo with his Maserati was considered too slow, and was not allowed to start).

It was Brooks, the quiet London dentist, who first turned heads as the stopwatches told their story during that first practice session on Wednesday evening at the Geux circuit. The current race lap record was 2min 24.9sec, recorded by last year's World Champion Mike Hawthorn in his V6 Ferrari. Brooks, however, on his first fast lap, went out and recorded 2min 21.8sec, but feeling he could go faster he went out again and set a time of 2min 19.6sec, averaging almost 133mph for the lap. This left the BRM and Cooper teams, in particular, realising that they must at least break into the 2min 20sec band to be anywhere near the front row of the grid. The Coopers were going well with Gregory getting down to 2min 20.8sec. Brabham and McLaren however, both had work to do if they were to improve. Moss had managed to get the sickly looking pea green BRM down to 2min 19.9sec after much effort, while the other BRMs could only get into the 2min 21sec margin. The second practice session only compounded the first, when Brooks put in a scintillating lap time of 2min 19.4sec, and Phil Hill a lap of 2min 19.8sec. Brabham had pulled out all the stops in the Cooper and split the two Ferraris with a lap in 2min 19.7sec.

This then formed the front row of the grid. In the second row was Moss in the BRM and Behra in the third Ferrari. Gurney and Gendebien could only manage the fourth row with the other two Ferraris, and had Schell and McLaren in the BRM and Cooper respectively in front of them. The two Lotus' of Graham Hill and Innes Ireland were behind, with the Cooper-Maseratis and 250Fs filling the rear rows.

Come race day the road and air temperatures were climbing as the sun got higher in the sky. So much so that, before the start, the drivers were allowed a free session to assess the condition of the track surface at places such as Thillois and Muizon, which were showing signs of breaking up under the intense heat. Drivers were dousing themselves and the cockpits of their cars with water in preparation for a long hard 50 laps that were to last for over two hours in those strength-sapping conditions.

The view down the long start and finish straight was one of shimmering heat rising from the road surface; distorting it so that it looked like a writhing black snake in the afternoon sun. 'Toto' Roche, as he had done so often before, was due to drop the flag to start the race at 2pm before running for dear life and turning the whole thing into a pantomime spectacle, which by now had become somewhat of a tradition. Just before the allotted time, the cars were formed up on the grid. As Roche dropped the flag and scurried to safety, so the crescendo rose to a pitch as the wheels of 20 cars spun and the tyre smoke poured from them. It was Brooks who, unsurprisingly, jumped into the lead and led down to the first right hand bend, with the rest of the pack scrapping in his wake. All that is, except Behra, who had been left on the line with a stalled engine.

Moss dived in to take second spot at the Thillois hairpin to slot in behind Brooks in an attempt to use his slipstream to try to break away from the howling pack at the end of lap one. By the end of the second lap the cars were beginning to string out already, with Moss being followed by Gregory, Brabham, Phil Hill, Schell, Bonnier, Trintignant, McLaren et al. At the end of the next lap at Thillois, Gregory flew past Moss' BRM. He was now off after Brooks, and set a new race lap record of 2min 23.8sec. This was swiftly followed by one of 2min 23.7sec on the same lap from Behra, who was rapidly making progress through the field. As cars accelerated out of the Thillois corner, pieces of tarmac were now beginning to fly off the wheels as if shot from a Roman ballista, hitting anything in their path – inevitably the following car, or in some instances, the driver.

Moss began to slip back now after being passed by Trintignant and Brabham: they had only just completed lap four, and so much had happened already! After five laps Brooks led the three Coopers of Gregory, Trintignant and Brabham, with Moss now occupying fifth place in front of Phil Hill, Bonnier, and Schell, before a gap to the next bunch consisting of Gurney, Graham Hill and McLaren, with Behra closing-in fast. The surprise so far was that instead of it being a comfortable Ferrari 1-2-3, the Coopers were really chasing hard and harrying the somewhat dated-looking larger cars from Maranello. Lap six and Trintignant slipped past Gregory into second place, followed by Brabham soon after. Moss then put in a lap of 2min 23.6sec, but this advanced him no further up the field. At this point of the race Scarlatti, Salvadori and Ireland had all been into the pits. In Ireland's case it was for new goggles, as his others had been smashed by flying stones and tarmac, which was now breaking up at a number of points on the circuit – a sign of things to come. Shortly afterwards Graham Hill also visited the pits after losing water when a stone had pierced his radiator ... the race was barely a quarter of an hour old! And still the sun beat down from a pitiless clear blue sky as lap by lap the track surface continued to deteriorate at an alarming rate.

The next driver in trouble was Bonnier, whose car had overheated out on the circuit as he approached Thillois. In spite of the heat, he started to push his car back to the pits. He was followed into the pits by Davis in the Cooper Maserati with a broken oil pipe. On lap eight it was Gregory's turn, and he came into the pits suffering from a gash to his face and heat exhaustion, and so his Cooper was pushed to the back of the pits after attempts to revive him proved futile. After 10 laps Brooks had a fairly healthy four second lead over Trintignant, who was doing a brilliant job with the Rob Walker Cooper. The Frenchman was noted for being a consistent, 'gritty' driver.

With Gregory now out of the running, Brabham and Moss were up to third and fourth places respectively, being pushed along by Phil Hill and Behra who had now claimed sixth place with a gallant effort after his poor start. But Gurney, Gendebien, Schell, McLaren and Flockhart were not too far away, and in a race like this anything can happen. On lap 12 it did, as Schell decided to do a bit of agricultural driving off-course. By the time he got back on the track he was a lap behind the leader, but he still kept going and would eventually finish seventh.

At this point in the race the fronts of most of the cars were peppered with stone chips and dents, their noses down to the bare metal devoid of all paintwork, while some had

Racing with Heroes

cracked or broken windscreens and their drivers with smashed goggles and cut faces, and there was still a good portion of the race to go. The only driver to be relatively safe was Brooks way out in front, but he still had to be wary when lapping slower cars.

On lap 29 Behra's valiant charge was to come to an end, for as he went past the pits a trail of smoke was seen coming from his exhaust – indicating something had blown on the left hand bank of his V6 engine – following which he slowed, allowing Moss to take the fourth position slot as he slipped back through the field. Behra managed to soldier on to complete only 32 of the 50 laps – just three short of the minimum number of 35 laps in order to be classified as a finisher.

The drivers were beginning to take as much of a hammering as the cars now. Flockhart, who had already had his goggles smashed by a flying stone, was subsequently hit in the eye by another, but still continued at pace, with blood streaming down his face, to take a thoroughly well-deserved sixth place at the finish, still on the same lap as the leader.

As well as the battering from flying stones and tarmac the remaining drivers were really suffering from the heat, with some trying to deflect a current of air into the car with their elbows, trying to stick their heads out of the side of the cockpit, or by raising themselves up in their seats, but the effect was minimal, for the rushing air stream was virtually as hot as that inside the cockpit.

By lap 36 Moss began to make an impression on the gap between himself and Brabham and Phil Hill in front of him. Moss had been trying to pace himself, for he had driven in Buenos Aires in 1955 as #2 to Fangio in the all-conquering Mercedes-Benz team in similar conditions, and he had obviously learned a lesson from the maestro on that occasion.

By lap 42 Gendebien disappeared from McLaren's mirrors after having a moment on the loose stuff, but he would eventually finish in front of the Cooper. On the next lap it was Moss who disappeared from the leaderboard. He had been having problems since early on in the race after cooking his clutch on the start line, and had done well to keep going as long as he had by changing gear without using his clutch. But after sliding on the moving morass that was Thillois, he could not help but stall the engine with the car stuck in gear. This made it impossible to push-start on his own, so he had to enlist help, knowing that he would be disqualified, but it was better than sitting it out or enduring the long walk back to the pits. It would also give him a chance to refresh himself for the Formula 2 race after the Grand Prix (this just wouldn't happen with today's Formula 1 teams and drivers). So Moss, within 7 laps of the end of the race, would join the growing ranks of those who would be classified as DNF on the result sheets.

Brooks carried on his serene way to the end of the race, much to the joy of Tavoni and the rest of the Ferrari team, for there would be few circuits on the calendar to suit them as well as this one.

The finishing positions then were as follows: Brooks in first place, with Phil Hill second, followed by Brabham in the Cooper third, Gendebien fourth in front of Bruce McLaren in fifth place, Flockhart, a gallant and bloodied sixth, was followed home by Schell, Scarlatti, de Beaufort, d'Orey, and the unlucky Trintignant in last place. This was all that remained running after two hours of the 21 cars that started the race. Fastest lap of the race was made by Moss on lap 40 (sans clutch), who then went on in the following Formula 2 race to win and make fastest lap again.

In the pits after the race the cars looked as though they had taken part in a demolition derby: battle-scarred and rather secondhand looking. The drivers looked just as bad: exhausted and dehydrated by the heat, tired by their efforts at the wheel of a 2.5-litre Formula 1 car for two hours, cut and grazed by the flying debris from the track. Thank goodness the next Grand Prix was in two week's time in England, where it would probably be raining, they all hoped.

So, at the end of a long, hot exhausting day it had been the quiet London dentist who had taken the winner's laurels. Tony Brooks – or Charles Anthony Standish Brooks, to give him his full name – was born February 25, 1932, at Dukinfield in Cheshire. He is a quiet, unassuming, slightly-built man, whose demeanour hid a raw natural talent. He seemed to excel on the faster circuits, and went on later that year to win at the Avus track in Germany. Unfortunately he was never lucky enough to become World Champion, but he undeniably had the ability to become one of the acknowledged elite. He is a much underrated driver, but to other drivers and teams he was a formidable opponent. His last Grand Prix was with the BRM team in the US Grand Prix at Watkins Glen in 1961. He will always be remembered as the man who started the dominance of British racing green by giving the Connaught team its one-and-only Grand Prix victory in the non-championship Syracuse Grand Prix in 1955. Since then British teams such as Vanwall, Cooper, Lotus and BRM, up to today's current crop of British champions, have continued to be in the vanguard of international motor racing.

Stirling Moss was once reported as having said, if he was to manage a racing team he would choose Jim Clark and Tony Brooks as his drivers. What greater compliment could be paid to such an outstanding driver?

Racing with Heroes

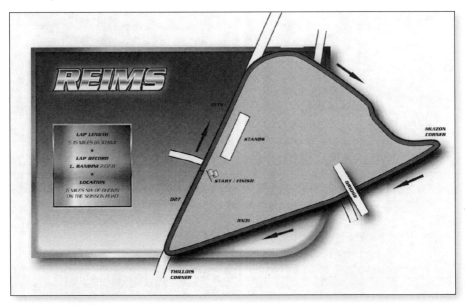

7 MILLE MIGLIA – 1955

A THOUSAND MILES TO VICTORY

THE early motor races which took place outside the United Kingdom were generally from city to city – such as Paris to Madrid, Paris to Bordeaux, and even Paris to Peking – run on public roads, commonly referred to as road racing. The last race of this kind to survive was the Mille Miglia. Its inaugural race took place in 1927 and its final race in 1957 after the tragic accident which killed the Marquis de Portago, his passenger, and ten spectators when he was less than thirty miles from the finish. The reason for the crash has never been conclusively proved, but it is thought to have been due to a burst tyre that was damaged in an earlier incident, a final drive failure, or simply a driver error.

Allegedly the race was conceived by five aggrieved young men, Giovanni Canestrini, Aymo Maggi, Franco Mazzotti, Flaminio Monti and Renzo Castagneto, after the Italian Grand Prix, which had been run around Brescia since 1922, had been hijacked and would in future be run at the Monza Autodromo, near Milan. They came up with the idea of a road race from Brescia to Rome and back to Brescia, a distance of some 1600 kilometres. This equates roughly to 1000 miles, and thus the Mille Miglia was born. Although it may seem strange for a country that normally measures distance metrically to name a race after the number of miles it consists of, it is a fact that the ancient Romans measured great distances in miles, so perhaps it's not so strange. The acceptance of the race's proposal by the powers that be was in part thanks to Mussolini's admiration and emulation of Adolf Hitler. He wanted his country not only to be a major world power, but a world leader (like Germany) in all respects; technologically as well as militarily.

Mille Miglia: the words conjured up wonderful emotive pictures in a child's imagination as he read through the description of the setting; the atmosphere, the preparation for the race, the unfolding dramas on the road, and the characters embroiled in those dramas. The pictures of the start and the oil, dust, and rubber-grimed faces of the tired but happy triumphant winners of this, the most gruelling and dangerous of modern races were indelibly printed in my mind.

'He who leads at Rome will not lead in Brescia.' This adage had always been true

Racing with Heroes

until now, for this year Stirling Moss and Denis Jenkinson proved that there is always an exception to the rule. For Moss, the local saying would have more than likely proved an additional challenge to be overcome. Denis Jenkinson, or 'Jenks' as he was affectionately known, was Moss' navigator for the event. He was, in fact, a motoring journalist writing for, amongst other notable journals, *MotorSport*, one of the most respected motoring publications at the time.

This was not however Moss' first Mille Miglia: that was in 1951, and by 1957 he had competed in six of these events, driven three Jaguars, and two Maseratis, as well as the Mercedes 300SLR. In 1955 Moss and the 300SLR were to reign supreme, for he also went on to win the Tourist Trophy race at Dundrod, the Targa Florio in Sicily, and the Swedish Grand Prix, which that year was for sports cars.

Among the previous winners of this prestigious race are such greats as Nuvolari, Caracciola, Biondetti (a four-times winner), Marzotto, Villoresi, and Ascari. The 1955 event, with its 520 competitors, of which just over half finished, took place under a cloudless sky on May 1-2, which, although making it warm work, was preferable to the rain-soaked races of some previous years, or the one the following year, which was run in atrocious conditions.

Moss was driving the very purposeful-looking 3-litre Mercedes-Benz 300SLR, as were Fangio, Hans Hermann and Karl Kling. These cars were capable of speeds up to 175-180mph. During the 1955 season, 300SLR cars had won five out of the six races entered, the sixth being the fateful 24 hour race at Le Mans where they were withdrawn after the horrific accident involving driver Pierre Levegh.

The 300SLR was, in effect the, W196 Grand Prix car retaining the straight-eight engine, albeit bored out from 2.5 to 3-litre capacity, but with a sports car body. Ferrari and Maserati were also fielding strong teams, with Castellotti, Taruffi and Maglioli being the main opposition.

Piero Taruffi, a grey-haired veteran at this stage of his career, was one of the favourites, and would be heading the Ferrari challenge consisting of two 3.7-litre, two 4.4- and one 4.5-litre car, the others being driven by Umberto Maglioli and Paolo Marzotto. In total, 18 Ferraris were to start this marathon, whilst Maserati went one better with 19 entries.

Some drivers took a navigator to help them, while others, such as Fangio and Castellotti, preferred to drive alone, feeling that this was an unnecessary weight penalty. Additionally, in Fangio's case, the death of one of his co-drivers during a Panamericana race during his formative years still weighed heavily on his conscience.

The cars started from the timekeeper's ramp in Brescia at one minute intervals, their start time reflected in the number given to each car. For example the Moss/Jenkinson car carried the number 722, indicating that their start time was 22 minutes past seven in the morning. Herman was in car number 704, Kling number 701, with Fangio being the first of the quartet to leave, with the number 658.

The smaller-engined cars, such as the Fiat Topolinos, started at 21.00 hours the day before, and the larger-engined cars followed in order of engine capacity. The entries were thus broken up into various classes, and this year – because of the large number of entries – there were no fewer than 27 classes.

The route of the race had been modified several times since its inception in 1926. This year's route took them eastward from Brescia across the plain of Lombardy to Verona, Padova, Ravenna, Pescara, through the Abruzzi mountains to Rome. At this, the half way point of the race, the teams would be able to refuel, the Moss/Jenkinson car taking on nearly 60 gallons of fuel, change tyres and make minor repairs, and if they were lucky, have time for a quick wash from a bucket of water to revive them.

From Rome they would start the second leg of the race northwards making their, by now, weary way through Sienna, Florence, and across the Raticosa and Futa Apenine passes before streaking through Bologna, Modena, Cremona and Mantua to finally arrive back in Brescia – providing they were lucky enough to make it that far. Mantua was not part of the earlier routes, but was included from 1954 onwards, following the death of the legendary Tazio Nuvolari the previous year.

Those evocative place names were only surpassed by the picturesque beauty of the scenery along the way. In places, the route followed the coastal road of the Adriatic, sparkling and blue in the spring sun. Elsewhere, the narrow roads cut through the towns and villages looking for all the world like something from a Renaissance painting. They also twisted their way through the hairpin bends across the Apennines with shear drops that would deter all but the bravest, or the most foolhardy of people.

Local drivers always have the advantage of being familiar with the course, or certain sections of it, as it is impossible to learn in detail a route of that length, and this is reflected in the list of past winners. This much was clear to Moss and Jenks as they drove the route in preparation for the race, and so they decided that they needed a "cunning plan" to stand any chance of winning. The 'toilet roll', or 'brain', was their solution. It consisted of a box, about the size of a shoe box, which contained a roll of paper incorporating their pace notes, which could be wound on from one roller to another as they progressed along their way. Sounds great in theory, but would it work in practice? Having the pace notes was one thing, but for Jenks to convey them to Stirling was another matter. The problem was resolved by the use of a variety of hand signals to overcome not only the roar of the engine, but also that of the wind as they rushed on their way at 170mph or more.

In February of that year, reconnaissance and testing of the car started, followed later by two more visits to record their pace notes. To acquire these pace notes it was necessary for the pair to drive the entire route of the race, not once, but a number of times, eventually clocking up in excess of 12,000 miles in the process. This was not unique to the Moss/Jenkinson pairing, as all the major teams had reconnoitred the route prior to the event. Jenkinson used kilometre marker stones and land marks as reference points for their reconnaissance notes. The one flaw in their preparation, however, was that they had taken their pace notes while travelling at a lower speed than they would in fact be travelling during the race itself. This meant that where a bend or brow could be taken flat-out at 130mph and recorded as such in the notes, it may well not be at racing speeds of 170mph. This would become apparent as the race unfolded.

During the race, the roads would be closed to the public. This was not the case for the reconnaissance runs, which Moss discovered when a horse and cart wandered into his path while travelling at speed on one occasion, and an army truck on another. Moss was not the only one to have problems in preparation for the race. Other drivers also had similar hair-raising stories. They had gone over their pace notes time and time again to refine them and ensure that they were as accurate as they could possibly get them, as an error could cost them time or even worse prove fatal. The drivers even practised changing the spare wheel and aero screens. The famous Mercedes-Benz preparation for the race left nothing to chance and was dealt with the typical Teutonic efficiency for which it was renowned.

They had scheduled 'pit stops' at Ravenna, Pescara, Rome, Florence, and Bologna. Complete spares were carried for the cars to enable them to replace virtually any part, as well as suitable sustenance until the next stop. Moss also made his own preparations, for he was about to set out on an Herculean task, to drive the whole 1000 miles as fast as he could – in fact faster than anyone before, or since. He would also have the additional weight handicap of a passenger. Having said that, if there is one thing that Jenks was not, it was a passenger. He was a very essential part of this well-oiled machine, something which Moss would be the first to testify. Moss' worry, if he had but one, was that he needed to maintain his high levels of concentration for the whole distance, which would be difficult. He did however acquire a little help from his friend, teammate and fellow competitor, Fangio, in the form of some 'stay awake pills,' which he took before the race. To this day he doesn't know what those pills contained. Probably some ancient South American ingredient, but they certainly seemed to work.

SO IT BEGINS

By 7.20am, most of the cars had already left Brescia, and only the larger-engined cars remained. With two minutes to go, Moss and Jenks were in their car ready for the off, with the morning sun beginning to rise in the sky, Moss adjusting his goggles and Jenkinson sitting with the 'brain' on his lap. As the seconds ticked away Moss engaged first gear; suddenly the starter gave the signal, and they were away down the ramp that was surrounded by spectators in the Viale Venezia. The meticulous Mercedes team had previously checked that the car would not bottom at the base of the ramp, being particularly heavy with its full fuel load at the start. The crowds surged forward as the car sped on its way, so much so, that Moss had to weave the car from side to side to clear a path as he accelerated up through the gears. With the tyres squealing on the cobbled roads of the town; they were on their way.

Within a short while he was already making up time on the cars that had left Brescia earlier, but Moss new that one of his biggest threats, Castellotti, who started at 7.23 with the big six-cylinder 4.4-litre Ferrari was behind him, and to stay in front Moss would have to drive like the wind. The weather was good and the car running well; Moss was in a confident mood. Jenkinson was settling down to the rhythm of the car, the rasping exhaust note, the ease and precision with which Moss controlled it, and the job in hand. This was in a day and age when two-way radio communication between team and car did not exist, and the drivers would be updated about their position and the opposition's only at the checkpoints along the route. In the meantime, all Moss could do was to keep the accelerator to the floor, whenever possible, and trust implicitly in Jenkinson's signals for the next ten hours or so. This was going to be no picnic.

By now they had left Brescia well behind them, and had already come across the wrecked remains of cars whose drivers had been trying just that little bit too hard and had come to grief at the side of the road. The car was really into its stride now, but the noise and fumes from the exhaust, together with the heat from the engine and the, at times, violent buffeting he was getting in the car, combined to make Jenks (putting it mildly) unwell. This was uncomfortable in itself, but was also disconcerting and distracting, and it could not have been easy for him to concentrate on his notes and give the all-important signals to Moss. Castellotti was indeed catching them (he had left Brescia one minute after Moss); he was hurling the 4.4-litre Ferrari around like a man possessed, the tortured tyres screaming at every turn. Here was a man who meant to leave his mark in the record books. With his Latin temperament spurring him on, he was catching the 300SLR of Moss and Jenkinson hand over fist. But could he keep it up? Could the car keep it up? The next few hours would tell.

It wasn't long before he had the silver Mercedes in his sights. As they approached Padova, Moss could see him bearing down on him in his rear view mirror. The sight must have momentarily distracted Moss, for as they entered the town Moss left his braking a fraction too late, and suddenly the car went into a slide. Fortunately, the car caught the straw bales, which did no more than dent the wing. In the meantime, with arms flailing and lights flashing, Castellotti tore past in a cloud of dust with a triumphant grin on his face. Moss simply found first gear and carried on in his characteristic unflurried driving style, but gradually saw Castellotti pull away and disappear into the distance, kicking up the dust and gravel as he went. He was really going for it and was soon out of sight. It must have occurred to Moss that no man could sustain that level of driving for long – something was bound to happen, and he wanted to be on hand to take advantage when it did.

On they raced to Ferrara, and from there to Ravenna where they came to the first time control point. Here, they would have their route card stamped, which they did as quickly as they could, barely stopping. Castellotti had reached the control point half a minute before them, and was nowhere to be seen. As Moss selected bottom gear and the tyres squealed under acceleration, they could just see a swarm of mechanics hurriedly changing the tyres on a Ferrari. To their amusement it was Castelloti's car, which had almost literally chewed up its tyres and was now once again behind the Mercedes and would have to get past all over again.

Racing with Heroes

They were now heading south on the coastal road towards Pescara with the Adriatic on their left, shimmering in the morning sun. Up until now everything had gone fairly smoothly, if smoothly is the right word. The pace notes had proven more than worthwhile – until that is, they approached Pescara, where they reached a brow, which, during their recce, had been noted as "flat out." But that was in the roadster at 120mph. As they breasted the brow at approaching 160mph, the car simply took off. Moss sat motionless during the flight, for he dare not turn the wheel, full-well knowing that it could mean disaster if the car regained the road with the wheels anything but in-line. Luckily, they made a clean four-point landing, gave one another a quick glance of relief, and carried on their way. They estimated afterwards that the car had travelled nearly two hundred feet while airborne.

Unfortunately, there was no time to slow and take in the breathtaking views, for Moss was aware that Castellotti would be doing everything he could to chase him down. Moss knew that Castellotti, being the proud Italian he was, wanted to win this race on his home soil badly. He also knew that Castellotti's Latin temperament could be his Achilles heel. On they swept through sun-baked villages and towns, leaving dust clouds in their wake. By the time they reached Pescara, Taruffi was in the lead ... just. Pescara was their first fuel stop. The Mercedes mechanics descended on the car like locusts; they refuelled the car and at the same time gave it a quick once-over, checking the tyres, cleaning the windscreen, and, just before the car left, even feeding our two intrepid racers with orange and banana slices. In less than half a minute the pair were on their way again. As they were leaving the town Moss missed his braking on a right hander, and the car slid out of control into some straw bales – luckily there was nothing more solid, although they dealt a hefty whack to the Mercedes front wing. It could only be hoped that no damage to the radiator or steering had been incurred. There was straw everywhere. Feeling slightly sheepish, Moss carefully drove around the remaining bales and back onto the road, with Jenkinson brushing off the odd strands of straw from himself as they went. Within seconds they were tearing along at unabated speed as though nothing had happened. On they drove to Popoli, and from there to the control point at Aquila where, once again, they barely stopped as their card was stamped, then they were off on their way, heading for the halfway point that was Rome.

"HE WHO LEADS AT ROME WILL NOT LEAD IN BRESCIA"

With headlights flashing and horn blowing they entered Rome, where the crowds were thick and spilt into the roads in their enthusiasm, so that Moss had to reduce his speed to 130mph. It had taken them just over five hours to cover the 540 miles from Brescia, and in doing so they had averaged approximately 107mph. It took the Mercedes mechanics just 60 seconds to refuel the car, change all four wheels, clean the windscreen, and for Moss to answer a call of nature. While stationary they learned that they were in the lead by some two minutes from the old fox Taruffi. But as they jumped back into the car and roared off once more, the adage of leading at Rome must have gone through Moss' mind. Would it prove true yet again? On they flew, hurtling past cars that had left Brescia hours before them, but travelling at a fraction of the speed of the Silver Arrow carrying the famous three pointed star on its bonnet. They also saw the remains of their sister car belonging to Karl Kling, wrecked against a tree after its driver had lost control attempting to avoid spectators who wanted to get a little too close to the action. Fortunately, Kling had escaped with his life, but had sustained a number of broken ribs, cuts and bruising in the incident. Moss didn't know this, however, as Kling had already been taken from the car. From the state of the car Moss could only guess at the fate of his teammate.

On they pushed, northwards towards Viterbo, and, as they did so, Jenkinson was distracted by a splash of fuel that had been blown against his neck from the slightly over-filled tank. Jenkinson missed the signal as Moss approached a tricky right hander. Suddenly, Moss was driving blind, without the aid of the directions he relied so heavily upon. Luckily, it was part of the course that they had covered on a number of occasions previously and Moss recognised it. Dark looks and a few well-chosen words from Moss were lost in the roar of the engine and the rushing stream of air that met them as they scrabbled round the corner. On and on they sped, there seemed no end to it, with Jenks sitting there stoically beside Moss, both concentrating on the job in hand for over six hours now.

Up and over the Radicofani pass, the car sliding in the turns beautifully under control, until that is, they approached the bottom of the pass. As Moss swung the car through yet another turn in the road, the car suddenly spun, and in an instant they were suddenly facing in the opposite direction, in a ditch with a large dent in the rear wing where it had thumped the bank. After the hundreds of miles of pushing the car to the limit the brakes had worn, causing them to snatch just as Moss entered the corner, and it was this that had made the car pirouette so swiftly. Once again luck was on their side and Moss was able to engage bottom gear and drive out of the ditch, but it had cost them time, and there were still the daunting Futa and Raticossa passes to come; the brakes were bound to deteriorate further by the time they reached them. The thought must have been unnerving to say the least for our intrepid pair.

The next control check point was Sienna, but, after leaving there, they still did not know how close Taruffi or any of their other rivals were to catching them, or if indeed they were in front of them in time, if not on the road. They just couldn't tell, all they could do was to keep going as fast as they could with the searing heat of the afternoon sun beating down on them. The ancient town of Florence was next, famous for its art galleries and the family seat of the Medicis, the Ponte Vecchio, and for being synonymous with Michelangelo Buonarroti. Across the bridge over the river Arno they streaked, and through the town, and again the townspeople were thronging the streets, leaning out of their windows, even climbing trees to shout out their encouragement to the pair as the car slid to a stop at the control point. Almost instantly they were off again in a blur of speed and sound, leaving the spectators wanting more as they watched the car disappear, leaving the old town with its cobbled streets and tramlines behind.

Racing with Heroes

The car was looking slightly the worse for wear now, and Moss and Jenks must have been beginning to feel the strain also, they had covered nearly 750 miles roughly three quarters distance. Now came the challenge of the Futa and Raticossa passes which Moss tackled the only way he knew how: as fast as possible. He averaged 60mph across the two mountain passes. He must have been aware that the brakes were now almost completely gone. In fact, when the car was checked over at the end of the race he had no brake linings left and they were operating metal on metal, which is no way to cross mountain passes at high speed. Was it inspired driving, courage or shear insanity? Call it what you will ...

Even on the mountain passes the people were out in force, cheering, shouting and waving the leaders on, although Moss and Jenks' were not aware that their main opposition, Taruffi was out of the hunt with an oil pump problem. It was on the Futa pass that they saw another of their team – it was the car belonging to Hans Hermann, but this time the car appeared undamaged, so Moss assumed it was a mechanical failure. On through what would normally be the quiet Italian countryside the silver projectile sped, past farms and small villages with Moss keeping an ever watchful eye. For although the roads were meant to be closed to traffic, he could never really be completely sure that some local had not brought his horse and cart, or tractor, or ageing Fiat out onto the road. Every now and again they would come across small groups of people at the roadside cheering them on, sometimes they would be aiding a competitor whose car had expired at the roadside, or even on some occasions helping to extricate a car from a ditch, together with its occupants. Still pushing on at great speed they arrived in Bologna with their now customary cloud of dust and screeching of tyres as they had their card stamped yet again at the control. Unfortunately, so hurried was their exit that they did not pick up the piece of paper that told them they were extending their lead over second place man Fangio. Off with a blare from the mighty exhausts of the Mercedes, they went on the road which would now lead them through Modena where Enzo Ferrari and the Maserati brothers had their factories. From Modena the road took them to Reggio and Emilia which gave its name to the road, the Via Emilia.

It was by now a very warm Italian afternoon, particularly so for Moss and Jenks. Who said Sunday was a day of rest? Still the countryside flashed by in a blur as they ate up the miles at 170mph. Still the multicoloured countryside flashed by with its parched earth and terracotta pan tiled-roofed sepia buildings, dried out under the heat of the Italian sun, On and on to Parma and to Piacenza. As the road unrolled in front of them, so did the roll of directions that Jenks had been clutching since they left Brescia early that same morning. Little did they know what a momentous drive they were to have that day; but it was not over yet. Still they were passing cars that had left Brescia before them, they had made amazingly good time in their much smaller-engined cars, and had managed to survive the gruelling course where others had failed. And, in typical fashion Moss would give them a wave as he went past to salute their outstanding achievements.

They now approached Cremona, the once immaculate Mercedes looking now battle-scarred and the worse-for-wear as it approached the end of its 1000 mile test of endurance.

Moss and Jenks weren't looking too pretty at this stage either. For the car that made the fastest time for the section between Cremona and Brescia, there was an additional award of the Nuvolari Cup. Mantua was in fact the last check point, and was just over 80 miles from Brescia. Moss must have felt that he was nearly home. He was still pushing hard, brakes or no brakes: after over 900 miles Moss, Jenks and the Mercedes were still giving it all they had. During that final section Moss' average speed was 123mph.

And so they entered Brescia like a triumphant Roman army. The crowds turned out in their thousands to line the route and salute a worthy winner in record time. Again Moss had to swerve the car from side to side with horn blaring to make a path through the tumultuous throng. Italians love their cars, their racing and their heroes.

TO THE VICTORS THE SPOILS

As they clambered from the car they were given the news that they had won. They could hardly believe it, after all the events and dramas of that ten hour trial. They were mobbed by fans and press alike. The car had done its job, the "brain" had done its job, and Moss and Jenks' had used the two to perfection. In fact, when the car was taken back to Stuttgart, the engine was tested and gave exactly the same performance figures as the day it was installed. What a testament to the Mercedes engineers and mechanics!

After just over ten hours the result was: 1st Moss/Jenkinson Mercedes-Benz 300SLR, 2nd Fangio Mercedes-Benz 300SLR, 3rd Maglioli/Monteferrario Ferrari, 4th Giardini Maserati, 5th Fitch/Gesell Mercedes-Benz, 6th Sighinolfi Ferrari.

Moss had become the first and only Englishman ever to have won this punishing event. What a day – a day that you or I, after having driven in the toughest race in the world, would have given all simply to relax and have an early night in bed to unwind from the rigours of the day, but not Moss. He simply took a hot bath, had dinner, and jumped into his Mercedes 220A and drove to Stuttgart to arrive for a lunchtime meeting with the Daimler-Benz directors the following day. Well, he had to do something I suppose until those little South American pills wore off. Jenks, meanwhile, had a race report to write like no other, after which he simply covered the typewriter, folded his draft, placed it into an envelope and posted it off to the *MotorSport* offices to catch the next post. What faith he must have had in the Italian postal system.

8 GERMAN GRAND PRIX – 1935

THE TORTOISE AND THE (MANTUAN) HARE

H E has been known by many names, including Great Little Man, Il Mantovano Volante (The Flying Mantuan), and Nivola, but his full name was Tazio Giorgio Nuvolari. He was born to Elisa and Arturo Nuvolari on November 16, 1892, and they lived in a small town called Castel d'Ario just outside Mantua in northern Italy.

Here was a driver in the archetypal mould – who could drive any type of car anywhere, and win. He was, in Enzo Ferrari's opinion, along with Stirling Moss, one of the greatest all-round drivers he had ever seen, while Dr Ferdinand Porsche is reported to have called him "The greatest driver of the past, the present and the future." He was only small, just 1.6m (5ft 3in) in height, and slight in build, but some believe him to have been the greatest of all drivers. He often wore a badge with the emblem of a tortoise pinned to his famous yellow jersey, given to him by the famous Italian poet and writer Gabriele D'Annunzio. He even had the same emblem painted on the cars he raced with such physical ferocity to win nearly 200 races in a career that spanned from 1920 to 1948. The war intervened, but when it was over he returned at the age of 53 to race again. He finally ceased battling against the odds when he died in August 1953 following a severe stroke.

He is often depicted throwing around the 16-cylinder Auto Union during the 1939 British Grand Prix at Donington, the monster of a car making him look diminutive, but he could bend that car to his will like no other driver, becoming airborne as he hurled it through the corners and the undulations of that narrow British circuit.

Not unnaturally with characters such as Nuvolari, legendary stories of his bravery, foolhardiness and stubbornness abound, such as the time during the darkness of the closing stages of the 1930 Mille Miglia, when tailed his rival, Varzi, for mile after mile without lights so that Varzi would not see him closing. Shortly before reaching Rome, Nuvolari put on his lights and accelerated past his rival with a grin on his face (much to Varzi's dismay) to win the race. Or there's the tale of the time he crossed the finishing line sans steering wheel, turning the steering column with a wrench to guide the car.

Like Alberto Ascari, Nuvolari began his racing career on motorbikes, becoming the

350cc champion of Europe in 1925. Being the fearless racer that he was, he often took tumbles that resulted in injury, but, even when encased in plaster, this never stopped him racing for long – usually against all medical advice.

During his early racing career with bikes and cars he raced against his friend, Achille Varzi. Friends they may have been, but as previously mentioned, they were fierce rivals on the track, and during the 1930 season both drove for the works Alfa Romeo team, the year that Nuvolari won his first Mille Miglia.

Nuvolari had a number of memorable races during his career that typified the man, his love of racing, and his never-say-die spirit. One such race was the 1935 German Grand Prix at Nürburgring, where he drove an Alfa Romeo P3 (that predated its opposition by four years) against the latest machinery Mercedes-Benz and Auto Union could produce. The Alfa Romeo was about 100hp down on all of the silver cars with it's 3.2-litre straight-eight engine. It was basically two four-cylinder engines joined in the middle, and was mated to a three speed gearbox. Above the deep engine note at racing speed could be heard the whistle of the twin Roots superchargers as the car bellowed its way around the circuit. In the German press it was rumoured after the race, that the engine was in fact 3.6-litres. Sounds like a case of sour Germanic grapes! Nine of the silver cars were lined up against him that day: five Mercedes and four Auto Unions to be driven by, amongst others, Hans Stuck, Rudolf Caracciola, Bernd Rosemeyer, and Manfred von Brauchitsch, as well as his old friend and adversary, Varzi.

As so often happens at the Nürburgring, the weather closed in before the race. The track surface became lightly spotted as the rain that had been threatening for some time crept in from the north. After just a few minutes the dappled ground resembled a mirror as the islands of damp patches became puddles and the puddles joined to form a moving glassy surface across the track and surrounding areas. The rain-laden clouds began to release their contents in large droplets, but this was not enough to dampen the spirits of the partisan home crowd. Germans from all over the country had thronged to the Nürburgring that day to watch their beloved silver cars imperiously beat the impertinent little red, blue and green cars out of sight. What could they possibly offer in the way of a challenge against the technological and industrial might of the Fatherland? Nuvolari; that's what they could offer, but would it be enough? What could one small man do against the giants such as Caracciola, von Brauchitsch, Rosemeyer etc? The rain continued to descend, making what was always regarded as a difficult track a very dangerous one – one to be treated with the utmost respect.

This legendary 14-mile circuit has produced many memorable races, such as the race in 1939 which was won by the Englishman Richard Seaman, who lost his life at Spa Francorchamp soon after. Or the 1957 epic three-way tussle between the Ferrari's of Hawthorn and Collins, and Fangio in his Maserati, to clinch his fifth and final World Championship. Or the rain-soaked, mist-shrouded race of 1968 won by Jackie Stewart, or the 1961 race in which, for the second time that year, Moss had humbled the great Ferrari team which had swept all before it, in his privately entered Rob Walker Lotus.

Racing with Heroes

The list is endless – Clark, Surtees, Caracciola – all have demonstrated their supremacy in the art of driving here and earned the title Regenmeister.

The Auto Unions to be driven by Hans Stuck, Achille Varzi, Bernd Rosemeyer and Paul Pietsch were all the latest B types with their enormous 5.6-litre V16 engines. The Mercedes W25s were a mixture of three 4-litre straight-eight and two 3.7-litre straight-eight engined models. The remainder of the field consisting of seven assorted Maseratis, five Alfa Romeos, three of which were entered by Scuderia Ferrari (including Nuvolari's), two ERAs, and one Bugatti.

Initially, no one amongst the reported 300,000 partisan spectators gave this little Italian in his old-fashioned-looking Alfa Romeo much of a chance against the latest technology that Germany could offer. But they should have known that Nuvolari was at his best when faced with a daunting challenge such as this. He relished being the underdog and was a master at turning an apparently hopeless situation into one of glorious victory against all the odds.

As the race start approached, the rain seemed to increase in intensity as the cars started to line up on the grid, making the ageing Alfas look even more antiquated in their bedraggled state. If the situation appeared hopeless to most, the thought hadn't occurred to Nuvolari.

Grid positions had been decided by ballot, with the front row consisting of Stuck (Auto Union), Nuvolari (Alfa Romeo), and Balestrero (Alfa Romeo). Shortly after the fall of the flag, Caracciola jumped into the lead. Caracciola had become an acknowledged master at the ring, and revelled in the wet conditions having already won the German Grand Prix in 1926, 1928, 1931 and 1932. He felt at home here, and by the time he had completed his first lap he already had a lead over Nuvolari of more than 14 seconds. By lap two things seemed to be going from bad to worse for 'the great little man,' for he had now slipped back to fifth after being overtaken, first by Rosemeyer then Fagioli and Stuck. Shortly afterwards however Rosemeyer was forced into the pits with a mechanical problem, allowing Nuvolari back up to fourth.

He was now beginning to get the bit between his teeth, and really wound up the Alfa to record the first lap time below 11 minutes on lap nine. In the process he wrestled his dinosaur of an Alfa past two of the sleek silver-bodied Mercedes to climb to second spot. Surely he couldn't take the lead? Already the confident smiles of the home spectators were beginning to slip into looks of disbelief. But by lap ten, the impossible happened as he went into the lead while Caracciola's car began to falter.

The race was far from over, however, as Rosemeyer, making up for his early pit stop, homed in on the flying Mantuan, just as the leading four cars came in for simultaneous pit stops to replenish fuel and tyres as the race approached the half distance mark. The efficiency of the Germans in getting the cars back in the race was typical of these well-organized, well-drilled teams, and in less time than it takes to tell, they were on their way again.

By contrast Nuvolari, hoping to make a quick stop, was frustrated by a faulty fuel transfer pump and the pit crew had to resort to the time tested method of using churns and a funnel to fill the Alfa's tank. After more than two minutes spent in the pits Nuvolari finally got back on to the track in sixth position: behind cars he had already passed. The delay at the pit stop seemed to bring down the red mist for Nuvolari, for he now began to drive as though the devil was chasing him.

In the course of the next few laps he passed not only the Regenmeister himself, Caracciola, but also Stuck and Fagioli. He was, unbelievably, now second again. Nothing was going to stop him now. He had his sights firmly set on winning this race, but with seven laps remaining he was nearly a minute and a half behind Manfred von Brauchitsch in the lead. Manfred himself was no slouch at the 'ring, and behind the wheel of the famed Mercedes he must have thought he had the race in his pocket.

The Achilles heel of the Mercedes however, was to be the rate of tyre wear which had caused problems on previous occasions. Nuvolari was now reducing the gap on every successive lap: the next lap he had reduced it to 1min 17sec, a lap later it was 1min 3sec. At the end of the penultimate lap, lap 21, stopwatches in the Mercedes pits told the team manager Alfred Neubauer that Nuvolari had now reduced the margin to just 30 seconds. But he must have felt confident that this was too much even for Nuvolari to overcome in the course of just one lap, or was he aware that von Brauchitsch's tyres were just about kaput?

The harder Nuvolari pushed, the more Manfred tried to respond. The more he tried to respond, the more his tyres deteriorated. With barely half a lap to the chequered flag, a rear tyre finally had enough of the constant cornering, braking and acceleration, and burst – allowing Nuvolari to pass serenely into the lead. The German spectators were dumbfounded and stood in disbelief, including a certain Adolf Hitler and his Nazi party entourage, who had come to see a walkover by the might of the latest German technology and efficiency. They were not best pleased with this little Italian who had come to spoil their day in his out-dated scarlet Alfa, with the prancing horse insignia on its bonnet (not to mention the tortoise!) In fact, the win was so unexpected that there was no music of the Marcia Reale to play for the winner. But (so the story goes), it just so happened that Nuvolari carried a copy with him for just such occasions. Thus it was, that the Italian National Anthem reverberated around the 14 mile circuit as the fastest tortoise in the world triumphantly had the winners laurels placed around his neck, while on his grimy face he wore a smile from ear to ear. From 1934 the Mercedes and Auto Union teams were sponsored by the Nazi party. By 1939 Mercedes had won six, and Auto Union four of the eleven Grand Prix that had taken place – but not in 1935, when Nuvolari was the only driver to win a Grand Prix without driving for one of the German teams.

9 ITALIAN GRAND PRIX – 1971

THE FASTEST RACE EVER

D UE to the nature of the circuit there have been many spectacularly fast and close races over the years at the Monza Autodrome, set in the royal park near Milan. All the great names have raced, won, even come to grief here. The likes of Alberto Ascari, Wolfgang von Trips, Ronnie Peterson and Jochen Rindt lost their lives here, but because of its rich tradition and racing history, it is considered by some – certainly in recent years – to be the home of motor racing. It is the one track, together with Spa-Francorchamps, that all racing fans must visit at least once before they hang up their stopwatches and banners and slip into the seventh age of man: becoming armchair enthusiasts and donning their tartan slippers in old age.

It is, of course, the spiritual home of the Tifosi, that ardent band of Ferrari fanatics. To this group of people, Enzo Ferrari was a god, the team a golden calf, and the prancing horse a crusading banner which they follow religiously. For them, anyone who drives a Ferrari to victory, especially on the hallowed ground that is Monza, is their hero, treading in the footmarks of Ascari, Caracciola, Nuvolari – even Nigel Mansell.

In the days before a racing car's utter dependency on downforce and diffusers, slipstreaming was the order of the day at circuits such as Monza. This is the art of obtaining a tow in the air stream of a car barely feet, or sometimes inches in front of you, at speeds of 180mph or more. In order to do this the driver requires supreme confidence, not only in his own skills but also of those of the driver in front of him.

In 1970 Jackie Stewart snatched victory after crossing the line just in front of a group of three other cars by little over a second. In 1953 Fangio, after a race-long tussle with Ascari, Farina and Marimón, took advantage of over-eagerness on the others' part at the last corner of the last lap, allowing him to slip by to take the flag.

Monza was built in 1922 by the Automobile Club D'Italia, reputedly in just over three months. It is a high-speed circuit, with fast, long, sweeping bends connecting the straights, and as if this was not enough there is the banked oval section that was built to extend the circuit and increase its average lap speed. Fortunately, or unfortunately, depending on your point of view, the banked section was last used for grand épreuves in 1961. As speeds rose and the surface deteriorated, it was considered too dangerous to use in later years, the cars taking a visible pounding as their suspension was pushed down onto the track by centrifugal force. With the suspension becoming virtually solid, every bump and joint in the track's surface would hammer the cars relentlessly as they pounded around at speeds approaching 200mph, lap after lap. The consequences of a tyre, suspension or steering failure in those circumstances doesn't bear thinking about.

BRM: THE CAR

BRM has had a chequered history since the team was first launched in 1952, as on paper the 2.5-litre V16 produced that year looked, and technically should have been, a winner. It certainly had a good turn of speed and handled well enough, but on numerous occasions in those early days it did not make it to the grid, or lasted for only a handful of laps due to a technical malfunction. It showed that it could run well a number of times in the hands of Fangio, Reg Parnell, Stirling Moss, José Froilán González, and the American Harry Schell, amongst others. Unfortunately, it only flattered to deceive, and more often than not left its driver frustrated, and with a long walk back to the pits to explain what had broken this time. It had originally risen from the ashes of ERA, famed for its success in voiturette racing and hillclimb events, thanks to the efforts of Raymond Mays and Peter Berthon, who wanted to see a car in British Racing Green at the forefront of international motor racing. During the following years the team had limited successes with different models at different times, such as the1959 Dutch Grand Prix with Jo Bonnier and Graham Hill during the '60s, and Monaco in 1972 when Jean-Pierre Beltoise brought home the car to the winners' circle for the last time after a chaotic wet race.

PETER & MURPHY

Every now and then a talented but relatively obscure driver makes his mark by being in the right place at the right time, and doing what he does best ... it's Murphy's law in reverse. Peter Gethin was just such a driver, and the 1971 Italian Grand Prix was the right place to be. He was the son of Ken Gethin, the jockey (who, not uncoincidentally, came from Epsom), and although he left his mark as he made his way up the ladder in motor racing, he was not a prolific visitor to the winners' rostrum in Formula 1. Still, he did make it to the top.

During the 1971 season he drove the Tony Southgate-designed BRM P160, at that time sponsored by the Yardley cosmetic company (and run in its own inimitable colour scheme), which, for this race, was fielding no fewer than four cars: one for the Swiss driver Jo Siffert, one for Howden Ganley, one for Helmut Marko, and one for Peter Gethin.

Stiff opposition was present in the form of Jackie Stewart and François Cevert in their Tyrrells, and there were also the Ferraris of Jacky Ickx and Clay Regazzoni; Mike Hailwood in the Surtees, and the two March cars, driven by Ronnie Peterson and Henri Pescarolo – not forgetting the ever unlucky New Zealander Chris Amon in the Matra Simca. A star-studded field if ever there was one.

Racing with Heroes

For this the 50th anniversary of the Italian Grand Prix, practice had been a fairly orderly affair, or as orderly as it can be in Italy. Until, that is, about 6.20 in the evening with about ten minutes of practice left, when everyone seemed to be out together in tight bunches trying to get a tow from whomever they could!

The BRMs did well in practice, with Siffert getting onto the front row of the grid in third spot next to Jacky Ickx. Amon had snatched pole after getting a tow from a bunch of cars which catapulted him across the line to clock a time of 1min 22.4sec (an average lap speed of approx 156mph), with Ickx nearly half a second slower. Siffert clocked a time of 1min 23.03sec, with Ganley trailing just over a tenth of a second slower to claim fourth slot on the grid, just heading the leading Tyrell of Cevert. Gethin and Marko made it onto the grid in 11th and 12th positions respectively, just behind Pescarolo.

Also worthy of note was Emerson Fittipaldi in 18th driving the Pratt and Whitney-powered gas turbine Lotus 56 which appeared a number of times throughout the season, also driven by Reine Wisell on an experimental basis, but was later dropped. And so at the end of the final practice session the first four cars on the grid were V12-engined, as may be expected on a circuit such as this where power is king.

Race day dawned, and with the preliminaries out of the way cars and drivers formed up on the grid. The one minute signal had sounded, the drivers were itching to get under way. They waited, and waited and waited, then, with a swish of the flag the race began, and down towards the Curva Grande they all hurtled as one. But there was a red bullet that beat the others to it, and it was Clay Regazzoni in his scarlet Ferrari who had made a lightning start from the fourth row to head the field on that first lap, closely followed by his countryman Jo Siffert in the BRM. They were side-by-side as they completed the lap. The other BRM of Ganley was fourth just behind Stewart. He had turned the tables on Cevert by jumping him at the start. This, however, was going to be a no-holds barred race, with a constant jockeying for position. To put it in the immortal words of Denis Jenkinson, "... it was Harry Flatters" all around the circuit.

By the time another three laps had been completed it was Ronnie Peterson in the lead, having come from nowhere, with Stewart now in second place, Siffert third, and Regazzoni now back in fourth, but they were so close it meant nothing. Average lap speeds were just over 150mph, which was bound to take its toll on the machinery before too long.

And so it did, for first into the pits was Helmut Marko with a rough-sounding engine in his BRM, which was to make him an involuntary pedestrian soon after. In fact, none of the front running BRMs were too healthy as their temperature gauges started to climb. It was a combination of the delayed start, the afternoon Italian sun, the almost constant full throttle required for the four long straights, and the fast sweeping bends of the Autodrome and the close slipstreaming that was getting very little cooling air to the radiators. So, Ganley and Siffert dropped back in the pack.

Continued page 81

Juan Manuel Fangio – World Champion 1953, '54, '55, and '57. Often considered the master of his art as well as a great sportsman and gentleman, both on and off the track.

Route map of the 1955 Mille Miglia.

Cover of the *MotorSport* anniversary edition, featuring Denis Jenkinson's report of the historic 1955 Mille Miglia.

Rear end of the Lotus 18 showing the Chapman-designed rear suspension.

Ginther and Bonnier follow Moss through Station hairpin during the early stages of the 1961 Monaco Grand Prix.

The overcrowded harbour at Monte Carlo, with boats belonging to the rich, the royal, and the famous.

Graham Hill – World Champion 1962 and '68. A great driver and personality. Not only a Formula One World Champion, but also winner of the 24 hours Le Mans, and Indianapolis 500 – the triple crown.

Jim Clark – World Champion 1963 and '65, and one of the most naturally talented drivers ever to grace the racing circuits of the world.

Jimmy Clark in the Lotus 49.

BRITISH GRAND PRIX
Brands Hatch
18 July 1970

Official Programme

Sponsored by
DAILY MAIL

4s.

The cover of the official programme of the 1970 British Grand Prix. How different things look forty years later.

Even after a hard day's work, a racing driver's job is not finished. Graham Hill signs autographs while leaving the Dutch Grand Prix and Zandvoort, 1970.

Yardley BRM driver Peter Gethin in the paddock.

The determined three times World Champion, Niki Lauda.

Jackie Stewart at the Lord's Taverners cricket match which regularly took place the day after the British Grand Prix.

AUTOGRAPHS

TEAMS

Grand Prix Drivers	The Lord's Taverners
Niki Lauda	Mike Parkinson
Graham Hill	John Blythe
Jackie Stewart	John Alderton
Patrick Depailler	Ian Lavender
Jody Scheckter	Colin Welland
Guy Edwards	Mick McManus
Jochen Mass	Bill Simpson
Tim Schenken	Nicholas Parsons
Tom Belso	Terence Hardiman
Denny Hulme	Ernie Wise
John Watson	Jack Robertson
James Hunt	Robert Pewell
Ken Tyrrell	Michael Jayston
Ronnie Peterson	Malcolm McDowell
Carlos Pace	Bill Pertwee
Mike Hailwood	Cardew Robinson
	Don Davis

Umpires: Mike Pearce, Bill Harvey
Scorers: Norma Upton, May Harvey

An autograph card signed by Graham Hill, James Hunt, John Watson, Jody Scheckter, Jackie Stewart, Niki Lauda, Mike Hailwood, and Clay Regazzoni, which was used to raise funds for the Lord's Taverners society at the cricket match.

James Hunt and Mario Andretti in McLaren M23 and Lotus 77 respectively.

James Hunt in the 1975 Hesketh, prior to joining McLaren for the 1976 season.

The unconventional and incomparable James Hunt.

Thirteen out of the last fourteen Formula 1 World Championships have been won by cars relying on Lucas Petrol Injection.

Lucas

Sunday, 18 July

Event 3

The John Player Grand Prix

For International Formula 1 cars as defined by the International Sporting Code, with engines running on pump fuel, having a maximum capacity of 3000cc and not more than 12 cylinders. Ninth round of the F.I.A. World Championship of Drivers and the International Cup for Formula 1 Manufacturers.

START: 15.00		76 Laps	199·6 miles

No.	Driver	Nat.	Car/Entrant	cc
1	Niki Lauda	A	Ferrari 312T2/Spa Ferrari SEFAC	2992
2	Clay Regazzoni	CH	Ferrari 312T2/Spa Ferrari SEFAC	2992
3	Jody Scheckter	ZA	Tyrrell-Ford 34/Elf Team Tyrrell	2993
4	Patrick Depailler	F	Tyrrell-Ford 34/Elf Team Tyrrell	2993
5	Mario Andretti	USA	JPS 77/John Player Team Lotus	2993
6	Gunnar Nilsson	S	JPS 77/John Player Team Lotus	2993
7	Carlos Reutemann	RA	Martini Brabham Alfa/Martini Racing	2992
8	Carlos Pace	BR	Martini Brabham Alfa/Martini Racing	2992
9	Vittorio Brambilla	I	March 761/Beta Team March	2993
10	Ronnie Peterson	S	March 761/March Racing	2993
11	James Hunt	GB	Marlboro-McLaren M23/Marlboro Team McLaren	2993
12	Jochen Mass	D	Marlboro-McLaren M23/Marlboro Team McLaren	2993
13	Divina Galica	GB	Surtees TS/ShellSPORT-Whiting	2993
16	Tom Pryce	GB	Shadow Ford DN 5/Shadow Racing	2993
17	Jean-Pierre Jarier	F	Shadow Ford DN 5/Shadow Racing	2993
18	Brett Lunger	USA	Chesterfield Surtees TS 19/Team Surtees	2993
19	Alan Jones	AUS	Durex Surtees TS 19/Team Surtees	2993
20	Jacky Ickx	B	Williams FW/Walter Wolf Racing	2993
22	Chris Amon	NZ	Ensign N 176/Team Ensign	2993
24	Harald Ertl	D	Hesketh 308D/Hesketh Racing	2993
25	Guy Edwards	GB	Hesketh 308D/Penthouse Rizla Racing with Hesketh	2993
26	Jacques Laffite	F	Gitanes Ligier Matra/Ligier Gitanes	2993
28	John Watson	GB	Penske PC-3/First National City Team Penske	2993
30	Emerson Fittipaldi	BR	Copersucar Fittipaldi Fd/Copersucar Fittipaldi	2993
31	Ingo Hoffman	BR	Copersucar Fittipaldi Fd/Copersucar Fittipaldi	2993
32	Lella Lombardi	I	Brabham BT 44B/RAM Racing	2993
33	Damien Magee	GB	Brabham BT 44B/RAM Racing	2993
34	Hans Stuck	D	March 761/March Racing	2993
35	Arturo Merzario	I	March 761/Ovoro Team March	2993
39	Henri Pescarolo	F	Surtees TS 19/Team Norev	2993

Reserves

| 40 | Mike Wilds (1st Reserve) | GB | Shadow DN 3B/Team P.R. Reilly | 2993 |
| 41 | Brian McGuire (2nd Reserve) | AUS | Williams FW04/Driver | 2993 |

Key to nationalities: A–Austria, AUS–Australia, B–Belgium, BR–Brazil, CH–Switzerland, D–Germany, F–France, GB–Great Britain, I–Italy, NZ–New Zealand, RA–Argentina, S–Sweden, USA–United States of America, ZA–South Africa.

The uncompleted lap chart of the 1976 British Grand Prix. It was that kind of day.

THE ___ TIMES

Opinion

The worst act of cheating in the history of sport

Simon Barnes

It is the worst single piece of cheating in the history of sport. We must accept that Renault, in refusing to defend its Formula One motor racing team against the allegation that one of its drivers was told to crash, is admitting that the allegations are indeed true.

That is to say that Nelson Piquet Jr, son of the eponymous three-times world champion, a young man desperate to make his mark on the sport and yet struggling to keep up with its demands, was told to have an "accident" at the Singapore Grand Prix last September.

As a result of his crash, Piquet's team-mate, Fernando Alonso, was able to win a race he would otherwise have not, taking advantage of the safety procedures that are laid down in Formula One. Piquet was sacked by his team in July for his failure to bring in the results they wanted and turned whistleblower.

After the usual bluster and cover-up, Renault — the company, not the Formula One team — has made its move. It will offer no defence to the charges and has parted company with the team principal, Flavio Briatore, and his No 2, Pat Symonds. That is what happens when leading commercial concerns get mixed up in sport: their ultimate goal is profit, not sporting success. They are in it for image. They want to be associated with glamour and success, while the faintest hint of sordidness and cheating is anathema.

Headlines that bring disrepute to the sport, prompted by Nelson Piquet Jr's alleged planned crash in 2009. (Courtesy *The Times* and Simon Barnes)

Moss driving a Porsche at the Goodwood Festival of Speed.

One of motor racing's characters: Murray Walker plays hide-and-seek at the Goodwood Festival of Speed.

Tony Brooks reunited with the Aston Martin DBR1 at Goodwood.

The beautiful Aston Martin DBR1, looking resplendent in British Racing Green.

The author in his pride and joy, his Tiger Cat kit-car, manufactured by Tiger Racing of Wisbech.

The next generation. My two-year-old grandson is already on the right track.

Lap 14, and Peterson was still in the lead, but now it was Cevert in second spot with Regazzoni back to third, while Stewart had dropped to fourth. Was he just taking a breather and cooling his engine? The answer came on lap 16 as he pulled his car out of the race with an engine that had simply had enough! It was now becoming clear that the pace was too much, for on lap 18 Ickx brought his Ferrari into the pits, shortly followed by the other Ferrari of Regazzoni. The Ferraris were fast, but just too fragile, it seemed.

Barely a third of the way into the 55-lap, high-speed extravaganza, on lap 25 it was all change at the front again as Mike Hailwood took up the challenge in his Surtees TS9 – two great names from the world of motorcycle racing. At this stage of the race, as they approached the halfway mark, Gethin was in seventh spot some nine seconds behind the leading pack, but in a race like this anything could happen, and for Gethin it was about to. But he had some hard driving to do in the meantime.

With his car now cooled down and rejuvenated, Siffert once again took up the baton at the front to lead on lap 28, but as things turned out, not for long. Siffert was struggling with his gearbox, only to have it finally jam in fourth which, on a circuit like Monza, is not appropriate for any part of the course, and he gradually slipped down through the field, eventually finishing in ninth position. Amon, meanwhile, looked like he might achieve his maiden Grand Prix victory leading Peterson, Hailwood and Cevert across the line, but it was nail-biting stuff as first one, then another ducked out of the slipstream of the car in front to slingshot past in an ever-changing pecking order. It looked at this stage as though the BRM team had shot their bolt, for both Ganley and Gethin had dropped off the leading pack as Ganley's engine lost some of its edge.

The race was three quarters run now, and, it seemed, would be decided in favour of one of the five frontrunners. The gremlin sitting on Amon's shoulder had other ideas, though. With barely five laps remaining, Amon chose to remove one of the disposable visor strips from his helmet, but so in doing the main visor also became detached. With the wind tearing at his face he was forced to slow, and almost simultaneously the Matra V12 in the back of his car lost revs and effectively put an end to his race. By lap 45 Gethin was just two seconds behind Ganley, and by lap 48 he was past and up with the leaders. Having caught the leading pack, Gethin was now slipstreaming his way past first one then another, until on lap 52 he led Peterson and Cevert across the line. He led again on lap 53, but the race was far from over, for they were all still in a tight bunch, swapping positions around the circuit. 'Harry' could not get any 'flatter.'

There were now only two laps left. Gethin bided his time, waiting for the right moment to make his move. The one thing he didn't want to do was be leading into the last corner, for he knew that someone would get the jump on him before the finish line. So, as Cevert and Peterson jockeyed for position coming into the last corner, each seemed to out-manoeuvre themselves as Peterson lunged for the lead, allowing Gethin to barge his way through, much to the annoyance and chagrin of Cevert, who thought he had it all sewn up. Gethin managed to come out of the Curva Grande in front, but all five drivers had the metal hard to the floor in the drag down to the finish line. Flash went the multicoloured BRM to take the chequered flag, closely followed by a blur that consisted of Peterson, Cevert, Hailwood and Ganley, with just 0.6 seconds covering all five cars. Amon finally crossed the line in sixth place some 30 seconds later.

The Monza Autodrome, or La Pista Magica as it is known by the locals, had yet again provided a scintillating race with the result in doubt until the drop of the chequered flag, as well as what turned out to be the fastest race on record. This was Gethin's one and only Grand Prix victory, although he did follow this up with a win some months later at the Brands Hatch Race of Champions, in a race that included Formula 1 as well as Formula 5000 cars, while driving his F5000 Chevron. He also had a victory in the same race the following year. Unfortunately this was marred by the death of his former teammate Jo Siffert, who crashed his Rob Walker-entered car which burst into flames on impact.

With the later demise of the BRM team, Peter Gethin slipped from the Formula1 scene, but while he was there he showed that (with a little help from Murphy), he had what it takes to become a winner in illustrious company. His last Grand Prix was the 1974 British Grand Prix, and his last race in 1977.

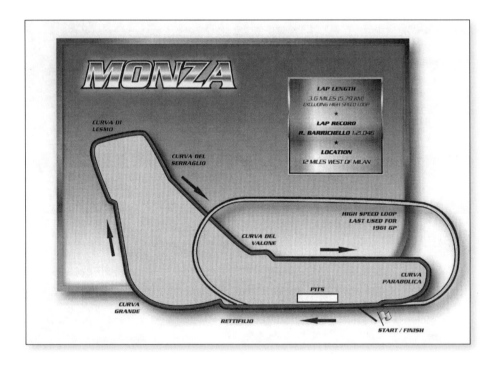

10 BRITISH GRAND PRIX – 1976

A WAVE OF BRITISH EMOTION

THE Brands Hatch circuit is a particular favourite of mine. Its setting, nestling as it does amongst the Kentish hills near Swanley, makes it a natural amphitheatre. It was one of the first circuits I visited, and to be able to see the whole of the original circuit from virtually anywhere around the course was, I found, particularly exciting. Watching a chariot race in Rome's Colosseum must have had a similar effect on those spectators, watching a similar sport, more or less, nearly two thousand years earlier.

To this arena one day came a young blond haired Englishman. In some ways, not unlike another young man twenty years before, by the name of Mike Hawthorn. This particular young man, however, went by the name of James Simon Wallis Hunt. He was born August 29 1947, the son of a stockbroker. Some saw him as petulant, some as spoilt, some as a bit of an oddball, some as accident prone; others simply as a great driver who, in his day, could beat the best.

He had the manner of a public schoolboy, which indeed he was, having been educated at Wellington. In his formative years as a racing driver in Formula 3 he had earned himself the nickname of 'Hunt the shunt' because of his numerous incidents and accidents. He came to prominence driving for the Hesketh team under the patronage of Lord Alexander Hesketh, who together with 'Bubbles' Horsley formed and ran this unsponsored team from their own very deep pockets. They initially forayed into the realms of Formula 2 together, with a March 712, racing against contemporaries such as Mike Hailwood and Ronnie Peterson. From the Formula 2 ranks they jumped into the world of Formula 1 in 1973. They were looked on as upstarts by the established teams. Rich upstarts, but nevertheless, upstarts. Until that is, they started to be competitive with Hesketh's own car designed by Harvey Postlethwaite, and then to win races. Together they won their first Grand Prix in 1975 in Holland at Zandvoort, although they had won a couple of non-championship races prior to that, including the Silverstone Trophy race. Alexander Hesketh was very patriotic, and the car's livery was red, white (predominantly) and blue. The team was renowned for its exotic parties, particularly those held on Hesketh's yacht when in Monte Carlo.

Racing with Heroes

Unfortunately, the money couldn't last forever, and eventually the fun days came to an end and the Hesketh team withdrew from racing in November 1975. Hunt had to find another team, but it was late in the year and most teams, although they would have liked him to drive for them, were contractually tied. But the fates conspired to give James Hunt a winning hand, for it just so happened that former World Champion Emmerson Fittipaldi decided to quit his position at McLaren to form his own Fittipaldi Copersucar sponsored team, thus leaving an opening and a golden opportunity that Hunt could not pass up. Hunt had seven victories during the course of the 1976 season, but the British Grand Prix was to be one of the most dramatic.

Race day dawned bright and sunny at Brands in 1976; a typical English summers day, if there is a such a thing. The summer of '76 was recorded as one of the longest spells of dry weather in the UK in recent history. It was a summer of water shortages and standpipes in the streets, talk of droughts – a member of parliament was even appointed to oversee the situation. It was a summer of long hot days and sultry restless nights.

The sky was bright blue with thinly woven white clouds high in the sky. By seven o' clock the place was beginning to buzz with activity. The overnight campers were rousing after what was probably a fairly sleepless night. Helicopters seemed to be everywhere, stewards were ushering in the early arrivals, food stalls were setting up, the shops were getting ready to open, marshals were getting a hearty breakfast inside them, for who knew when their next chance to eat might be. A rich perfume of culinary delights began to fill the air, wafted by a gentle breeze. All morning streams of cars and swarms of spectators descended on the small Kentish circuit. The enclosures and stands began to fill until it seemed no more could be contained within its boundaries; but still they came. It was estimated that in excess of ninety thousand spectators turned out on that glorious summers day. Little did anyone know what uproar and confusion was to lay ahead later that afternoon.

The whole season had been packed with tension, disputes and drama. The two main rivals were James Hunt the English public school playboy and Niki Lauda the no-nonsense Austrian and current World Champion. During this season, Hunt was driving the McLaren M23. The M23 had made its debut in the 1973 South African Grand Prix with Denny Hulme at the wheel. It had been designed by Gordon Coppuck and John Barnard. Lauda was driving the T2 version of the Ferrari 312. Both drivers were supported by talented teammates; Hunt by the young German driver Jochen Mass, and Lauda by the Swiss-Italian Clay Regazzoni, who was to go on to give the Williams team its first Grand Prix win in 1979.

At this point of the season Hunt's and Lauda's championship tally of points were 26 and 52 respectively. It didn't look too good for Hunt, with only half the number of Lauda's points. Whereas he had four wins, two seconds and a third, Hunt had won in Spain and France only, taking second in South Africa and a fifth place in Sweden. Lauda was a shrewd driver who new how to play the percentage game. Hunt's win in the Spanish Grand Prix had the shine taken from it after he was disqualified for a technical infringement. He was later reinstated, but this was a glimpse of things to come later in the 1976 season.

During Friday morning practice, however, Jody Scheckter (the South African driver) was very fast, as he always was at Brands Hatch, and during that first session set a time that was just 0.01 seconds slower than Hunt. In the afternoon session, when the track was warmer and quicker, Hunt went on to record a time of 1min 20.30sec, just over 117mph. As was tradition, Hunt duly earned himself 100 bottles of champagne for being fastest man of the day. Second fastest during that second session, and putting himself next to Hunt on the grid was the indomitable Niki Lauda with a lap of 1min 20.50sec.

Scheckter, who was driving the ground breaking Tyrrell six-wheeler and who earlier had been very close to Hunt's time, got wide at Dingle Dell and shunted the bank quite heavily; so much so, that he had to revert to the old four-wheeler for the remainder of practice. A mechanic's life is not an easy one, and the lot fell to them to get the car repaired for the race itself, which they duly did.

For the second day of practice Hunt really put the hammer down to go even faster with a lap of 1min 19.14sec, while Lauda squeezed in a lap of 1min 19.35sec, with his teammate Clay Regazzoni third quickest after recording a time of 1min 20.05 sec. The front row of the grid was thus made up of Hunt in the McLaren on pole with Lauda and Regazzoni next to him in their Ferraris.

As the cars rolled out to their grid positions there was an extra edge of tension – more than usual it seemed. As the seconds ticked by and the drivers sat nervously in their cars awaiting the drop of the flag, the sound of the engines rose to a crescendo, the crowd was on its toes, people craning their necks to be sure not to miss a thing. Then, in a split second, the flag had dropped, and, as one, the drivers let in their clutches and they were off, scampering down to the first corner Paddock Hill bend, the tricky right-hander with an adverse camber which throws the cars to the outside of the track as they exit the turn, but they did not reach it. Suddenly there was a scarlet blur as the two Ferraris touched. In their wake all was chaos, as first Hunt, in trying to avoid the mêlée in front of him, was hit from behind, tipped onto two wheels, and was lucky to have not overturned. Behind him, cars were all over the place as they tried to avoid the unfolding carnage in front of them. At this point the race was officially stopped.

The cars that could made their way around the lap after tip-toeing through the wreckage to either call in to the pits, or to reform on the grid for a delayed restart. Hunt however, with his damaged car, was close to the pit lane and took this to get the car checked over and repaired. Unfortunately, this was seen as a breach of the rules that stated cars should complete the lap before going into the pits, as to do otherwise would entail travelling in the wrong direction in the pit lane. During the delay before the restart Hunt's mechanics worked feverishly to get the car repaired, which they did, just in time. The race stewards, however, felt that Hunt and the McLaren team's actions were illegal, and via the public address system announced that he would not be able to rejoin the rest of the cars on the grid.

Racing with Heroes

While all this was going on the crowd was getting hot, frustrated and impatient and began to vent its anger in a way completely unheard of before at a motor race in this country. It started with whistles, then slow hand claps, then boos. The clamour got louder and spread from stand to stand and to the whole of the enclosures. One might expect this sort of reaction in South America or Spain, or Italy even, but not in Britain. It just doesn't happen here. With the announcement of the impending penalty to Hunt the clamour rose to a howl, then drink cans and programmes were thrown onto the track. The race officials could see they had a problem: this could get out of hand. An announcement was made declaring that the race would be run with Hunt, but events leading up to and after the incident would be subject to a post-race review. This seemed to pacify the crowd, and as quickly as it had started, so the revolt subsided, but now the track had to be cleared of the debris before the race could recommence.

In the meantime the swarm of mechanics around Hunt's car had repaired the suspension damage, and the two Ferraris had been repaired in time to take their place on the grid as before. Laffite in the Ligier, however, did not, as the front of his car had been comprehensively wrecked when he rammed the guard rail during the mêlée.

For the second time that afternoon the flag was dropped and the British Grand Prix was under way. This time Lauda dived to the front and led at the end of the first lap with Hunt and Regazzoni in close attendance in that order. Scheckter was in fourth with Arturo Merzario in a March Ford behind him in fifth. As Lauda and Hunt tussled for the lead they proceeded to break the lap record on nine separate occasions between them over the ensuing laps, and in so doing pulled out a gap from the rest of the field. On lap 37 Regazzoni was in the pits with suspected oil pump failure. Merzario also went into the pits shortly after on lap 40. Hunt soon began to put the pressure on Lauda and the spectators rose to the occasion, cheering and spurring him on. By lap 45 he was trying to get past the wily Austrian. Then, at Druids bend, he lunged up the inside. There was nothing Lauda could do about it without taking the pair of them off the circuit. Once past, Hunt tried to shake him, but Lauda is no quitter and he stayed with him, until that is, his gearbox started to malfunction, making it difficult for him to keep the pressure on Hunt. Hunt began to pull away quickly now, and by lap 60 he had a 40-second lead. The crowd was in its element, willing on Hunt.

Scheckter was holding a solid third spot well behind Lauda, but equally well in front of Gunnar Nilsson. Nilsson was driving the John Player Special, but not for much longer, for as he approached the start/finish straight his engine blew, putting an end to his day of racing. Nilsson was to go on the following season to win at Zolder in the Belgian Grand Prix, but not here; not today. This promoted the Ulsterman, John Watson in the Penske Ford to fourth place, followed by Tom Pryce and the Australian Alan Jones in sixth spot, who was to become World Champion with the Frank Williams team in 1981.

The drama did not end with the fall of the chequered flag and Hunt climbing the rostrum to take the victor's laurels, for an objection by Ferrari to Hunt's actions following the shambolic start had been upheld by the authorities, and some weeks later Hunt was stripped of his points which was to put him under pressure during that rain-lashed final round run in the shadow of Mount Fuji at the Fuji Speedway circuit in Japan. Between these races came Niki Lauda's horrifying accident, which nearly brought his life and brilliant racing career to a premature end. As stated earlier, Lauda is no quitter, and in spite of having been given the last rites by a priest at his bedside, he recovered, and six weeks later was behind the wheel of the Ferrari 312 T2 again for the Italian Grand Prix.

As the season ended it was Hunt who won the battle for the championship, but Lauda who had won the battle for his life, and would again go on to win the title the following year. Hunt's turbulent life continued to have its ups and downs, both on and off the track. He scored his last World Championship points in 1978 and retired midway through the '79 season after just seven races. Following this he teamed up with Murray Walker to form BBC's Formula 1 commentary team. This at times was a lively affair, as the two of them did not always see eye-to-eye about what was happening on the circuit, but with their chalk and cheese attitudes they became a firm favourite with the viewing public. Unfortunately, in 1993, at the frighteningly early age of 45, Hunt died from a massive heart attack.

Many people have different opinions of James Hunt, but having met him briefly following the 1976 British Grand Prix during the Lord's Taverners charity cricket match, he came across simply as an unpretentious, modest person who had his own way of doing things.

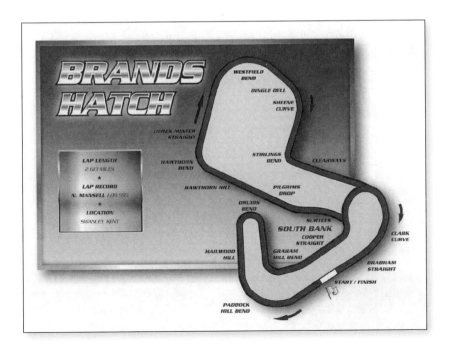

11 FRENCH GRAND PRIX – 1961

A STAR IS BORN

O CCASIONALLY, a shooting star bursts upon the scene – whether it be in politics, entertainment, industry or sport – writing his name large in the firmaments of history, but as all too often happens, he disappears just as quickly. Such a shooting star was one Giancarlo Baghetti ,who arrived with a resounding bang on the scene of international motor racing in 1961. Until the 1961 Syracuse Grand Prix, few had heard of this unassuming 26-year-old from Milan. The Syracuse Grand Prix was a non-championship Formula 1 race which acted as a curtain-raiser to the European rounds of the Formula 1 World Championship. It was run on everyday public roads amid the orange groves of this Sicilian town. The scent of orange blossom mixed with the smell of hot oil and exhaust formed a pungent aroma, one which no doubt the previously successful British racing teams will remember as a portent when looking back on the Grand Prix season of 1961. The 1961 Syracuse Grand Prix had been easily won by the hitherto unknown young Italian driver Giancarlo Baghetti from the Porsches of Dan Gurney and Jo Bonnier after the three works Ferraris had encountered various problems. He had risen through the ranks of Formula Junior and Formula 2, and now had wiped the floor with current Formula 1 contenders. He had also won second time out in Naples, but the French Grand Prix was to be his first championship Grand Prix. He was to drive one of the new, very striking, shark nose Ferraris which, as stated earlier, had stolen a march on the other teams when the new regulations were introduced for the 1961 season. BRM, Lotus, Cooper etc were to spend the rest of the season trying to catch up. The only driver who seemed capable of keeping up on some circuits was Moss, but on the high speed circuits even he had no chance of staying with the more powerful cars from Italy.

THE VENUE

The 1961 French Grand Prix was held on the roughly triangular circuit at Reims in the Champagne region of France, home to such famous names as Taittinger, Veuve Clicquot, Piper-Heidsieck and Mumm. Like most circuits it had evolved over the years, and its shape had changed. In its early days it was known as the Reims-Geux circuit because its layout took in the small town of Geux (with the circuit passing between the town's duck pond and the local grocers) on its route, but in 1952 it was re-planned to bypass the town.

The city of Reims is famous for its cathedral, with its Marc Chagall-designed windows, in which the Kings of France were once crowned. The French Grand Prix had been held at this circuit since 1925, and its last was in 1966, which was won by another young Italian by the name of Lorenzo Bandini driving a Ferrari 312, and setting a never to be beaten lap record of 142.15mph in the process. It was a high-speed circuit, and one which the Scuderia Ferrari team must have thought would give them an easy win.

The Porsche team, running their flat-four air-cooled engines however, also seemed well-suited to this circuit, and with their driver line up of Jo Bonnier, Dan Gurney and De Beaufort, would give the Ferraris, to be driven by Wolfgang von Trips, Phil Hill, Ritchie Ginther and young Baghetti, a run for their money. Baghetti's car was not in fact an official works team car, but one that had been loaned to a racing stable called Federazione Italiana Scuderie Automobilistiche, or FISA, as they were known, who were set up to give up-and-coming young drivers experience of Formula 1. This would then allow them to graduate to the Ferrari works team. It thus acted as a proving ground for the young hopefuls.

These then were some of the main protagonists of a field of 26 cars present for this Grand Prix. Other contenders were Lotus with their two car team for Jim Clark and Innes Ireland. Likewise, BRM had a pair of cars for Graham Hill and Tony Brooks. Again Cooper's two Coventry Climax-engined cars were to be driven by Jack Brabham and Bruce McLaren, while Moss of course had the Rob Walker Lotus, but this time it was the newer 21 and not the older 18 model, which he had brought home to victory so magnificently at Monaco a few weeks earlier. He had never won the French Grand Prix for some reason, could this be his year? It looked doubtful at that moment.

The rest of the field was made up of two Yeoman Credit Coopers for Surtees and Salvadori, two UDT Laystall Lotus' for Taylor and Bianchi, Lewis and Collombe in Coopers, Burgess, May and Mairesse all in Lotuses, and Scarlatti in a lone De Tomaso-Osca forming the remainder. During practice the Ferraris had easily outpaced the rest of the field, with all three team cars getting below 2min 30sec for the 5.1 mile lap, with Phil Hill completing a lap in 2min 24.9sec to take pole position.

Baghetti, his first time at the track, put in a very creditable lap time of 2min 30.5 sec with the 60 degree-engined version of the type 156 to put him on the fifth row of the grid. Moss was fourth fastest with a time of 2min 27.5sec. He managed this by tucking in behind the Ferraris while they were going for a quick lap to get a tow from von Trips. As soon as the Ferrari team manager Tavoni realised what was happening, he called his team in and was very careful when he allowed them out after that. Monte Carlo was obviously still a sore point. Clark put in a great effort to be next quickest with a time of 2min 29sec. During the second practice session Ferrari were aware that the others couldn't approach their times, and only Ginther went out.

Racing with Heroes

The final practice session provided no further surprises with Ginther the only Ferrari driver to improve his time to qualify for third place on the three-by-two-by-three grid of 26 cars. The two Porsches had qualified in ninth and 13th positions on the grid and did not look quite as competitive as they had in Syracuse. The Ferraris looked strong, and after their recent successes in Holland (Zandvoort) and Belgium (Spa-Francorchamps), seemed assured of another runaway victory on a circuit which suited them down to the ground. They were probably popping the corks of the locally grown champagne the night before the race in anticipation of victory.

So, for the third Grand Prix running it was an all-scarlet front row comprising Hill on pole, von Trips second, and Ginther on the outside of the front row. Credit should go to Moss and Clark (side-by-side on the second row, albeit nearly 0.3 and 0.5 seconds respectively off Hill's pole time of 2min 24.9sec) for being able to stay with the Ferraris as well as they did on a circuit that was ideally suited to the superior power of the Scuderia.

The race was to be run over 52 laps, a total race distance of 267 miles. From the start, the cars would accelerate down to the fast long right-hander taken at 160mph, and on to the short straight that led to the Muizon corner hairpin. Then they would power up through the gears along the one-and-a-half mile-long straight, with just the faintest of kinks about a third of the way down, until they approached Thillois hairpin. This was another tight right-handed hairpin bend that led on to the start/finish straight to begin another lap. Not technically a difficult circuit, but one that had experienced its share of surprises in the past, such as the 1953 race when newcomer Mike Hawthorn beat the World Champion Fangio in an epic wheel-to-wheel duel that will long be remembered. Similar to Monza, Reims was a power circuit, and one where a tow from the car in front using the slipstreaming technique would help the slower car to stay in touch, providing he didn't lose the tow.

THE STAGE IS SET

It was traditional that Toto Roche had the honour of dropping the flag at the start, which was also traditionally a shambles, as he persisted in doing it in his own inimitable way, year-after-year.

On this particular occasion the 'thirty seconds to go' board was hoisted barely five seconds after the one minute board had been held aloft, and the flag was dropped nine seconds later, as Toto scrambled to safety amid the clamour of 26 cars leaving the grid at high speed. As they sped towards the long right-hander after the start, it was Phil Hill from von Trips and Ginther with Moss, hanging on to their slipstream for all he was worth.

And so it remained for the first three laps until Ginther spun on lap four, forcing Moss to take evasive action, closely followed by Surtees who was unable to do the same and couldn't help clipping the spinning Ferrari. Unfortunately, this damaged the Cooper's suspension, bringing Surtees' race to a premature end. In the mêlée Moss moved up to third with Ginther racing back in an effort to reclaim the position. This leading bunch were beginning to break away from the charging pack, which consisted of Clark and

Ireland in the works Lotuses, with Gurney and Bonnier close behind, then McLaren and Baghetti, with Graham Hill pushing hard. It was all very frenetic as this group jostled for position at high speed down the long straights in their efforts to stay with the leaders. Baghetti hadn't got off to a particularly good start and initially lay in 14th spot, but was slowly working his way through. Hill led the scarlet charge for the first 12 laps before von Trips took up the baton, with Hill falling into second spot, by which time the Ferraris were 1-2-3 again as Ginther reclaimed third from Moss. Baghetti had squeezed himself into fourth place in that jostling pack by lap ten, and Moss was desperately trying to stay with him. Moss however had his hands full with a steadily deteriorating brake, which first let Clark then Ireland get between him and the Ferrari. From then on Moss was only going in one direction as he slipped backwards through the field.

So it was the Ferraris filling the first four positions. 'Here we go again,' was the thought on everyone's mind – until lap 19 that is, when von Trips pulled into the pits with the ominous sign of water issuing from the car's exhaust pipes. Hill was thus once again back in a comfortable lead from Ginther, while Baghetti was still being hounded by the pack led by Clark. Jack Brabham had pulled out of the race on lap 13 with a seizing engine. Moss eventually pulled into the pits to have a brake pipe replaced, but this was to be his final undoing, for while the car stood in the pits, molten tar collected on one of the wheels, putting it out of balance.

It was at this stage of the race that the silver cars from Stuttgart made their move. First Gurney and then Bonnier passed the two Lotuses, as one after the other they both fell victim to the loose debris of the ailing track surface, Ireland with a stone in his carburettor intake, and Clark with a stone smashing his goggles.

With the race now well into its second half a second blow struck the prancing horse, as Phil Hill also fell foul of the deteriorating track conditions as he spun on the slippery surface at Thillois, and apparently collected Moss in the process. Unfortunately Hill stalled his engine, which he was then unable to restart on the starter. By the time he had push-started it he had lost valuable minutes, and thereafter was never again in contention. Moss on the other hand had broken another brake pipe in the incident with Hill, which finally put an end to his days driving amongst the French vineyards. The whole character of the race had now changed thanks to the fickle hand of fate, which still had a few more tricks to play in the course of this midsummer's drama ... or would it turn into a French farce?

Ginther now found himself in the lead: could this be the day the diminutive Californian clinched his first Grand Prix win? The question was answered on the next lap as he too rushed into the pits, this time with low oil pressure, but he was sent on his way, as the current regulations forbade additional oil during the race. Tavoni knew that Ginther's race was run, and sure enough half way round the lap Ginther limped off the circuit with zero oil pressure.

The crowd was beginning to wonder what would happen next: it seemed the heat was getting to everybody, the spectators, the drivers and the cars alike. Baghetti, Gurney and Bonnier were now scrapping for the lead and it had turned into a real dogfight. The two

Racing with Heroes

more experienced drivers were now really putting the squeeze on the newcomer, with the lead changing from one lap to the next, each of them taking it in turns to be at the front. Meanwhile Tavoni and the rest of the Ferrari team were encouraging the youngster from the pits; shouting, waving, gesturing; willing him on. There were still ten more laps to go, and still the leading trio scorched past the pits as though tied together.

With three laps to go they were still at it hammer and tongs, this time with Baghetti and Gurney crossing the start/finish line side-by-side, wheel-to-wheel, when suddenly Bonnier's car started to trail smoke; not the thin wispy kind, but thickening blue smoke. He came into the pits, his race all but run. After a short stop he limped on to finish, but was no longer in the fight.

It was now just the two of them: Baghetti and Gurney, the Italian and the American, Ferrari and Porsche, and for the last two laps they slugged it out, trading places all the way around the circuit. As they started their last lap, once again they were side-by-side. Baghetti edged past the Porsche as they took the right-hander after the start, but Gurney was past again as they approached Thillois. When they exited the corner they did so almost abreast, with Gurney just having the edge.

Baghetti now made his move and judged it to perfection; a perfection which belied his youth and inexperience. He tucked in close behind the Porsche for the final drag down to the finish line, and using the extra revs that he had kept in reserve, he pulled out and catapulted past the silver car to win by less than a car's length.

Over a minute later Clark and Ireland crossed the line, followed by McLaren in the Cooper and Graham Hill in the BRM, with Bonnier making it home in seventh.

So Baghetti, driving the same loan car that he had won the Sicilian Grand Prix with, had now also won the French Grand Prix, and deservedly so. The young Milanese wrote his name in the history books that day: the only driver to win his first ever World Championship Grand Prix.

12 DUTCH GRAND PRIX – 1967

CLARK AND THE COSWORTH V8

JIM Clark was one of the most naturally talented drivers to sit in a racing car; he could make his car go faster than any one else. It didn't matter whether it was a Lotus Cortina at Brands Hatch, a Colin Chapman special at Indianapolis, or a Formula 1 car on any of the world's great Grand Prix circuits; if the car held together, he was invincible. He was also one of the safest drivers around, which is why his untimely death came as such a shock to the racing world. His natural ease in the car and his effortless driving style made him a joy to watch. He was born in Kilmany in 1936: six years later he and his family moved to Duns. From his quiet beginnings as a Scottish border farmer, Clark very quickly made his presence felt on the racing scene after racing sports cars in various local events. He also went on later to drive in the 24 hour race at Le Mans with the Border Reivers team. He came to the attention of Colin Chapman, who owned and ran the Lotus racing car company, while testing one of his cars as a prospective customer. He teamed up with Colin Chapman early on in his racing days and drove only for him during his Grand Prix career. These two were men of their times, for Colin Chapman was just as much a genius of design and innovation as Clark was a genius behind the wheel: theirs was a match that was destined to be.

Chapman had many other great drivers drive his cars such as Graham Hill, Mario Andretti, Jochen Rindt, Ronnie Peterson, and Innes Ireland, but there was never the same chemistry as there was with Clark. The third ingredient in the mix was the team of Keith Duckworth and Mike Costin, who had produced the Ford Cosworth V8 DFV that went on to become the most successful Formula 1 engine ever produced, which together with its derivative versions went on for 23 seasons. The DFV by the way refers to its double 4-valve arrangement. It was a V8 configuration and of 3-litre capacity to comply with the Formula 1 regulations of the time. It was designed, developed and built on an initial budget of £100,000 and was subsequently sold as a customer engine to numerous teams for years to come.

The Lotus 49, with its 3-litre Ford Cosworth V8 engine, and Jim Clark were what could only be described as a dream team, and together with Graham Hill as teammate, looked on paper to be unstoppable. Unfortunately after a promising start to the partnership at Zandvoort the season of 1967 did not go too smoothly. At Spa, in Belgium, Clark could do no better than sixth, and retired in the French Grand Prix that followed. He went on to win at Silverstone in the British Grand Prix but then retired in the next two outings at the Nürburgring and Mosport Park in Canada. Things then picked up again with a third place in the Italian Grand Prix, and wins in the last three races of the year at Watkins Glen, Mexico City and finally at Jarama in Spain. It was certainly a season of ups and downs.

Although Clark had seen construction of the new car in progress there had been no time for shakedown trials or testing. Any testing carried out was done by Graham Hill. It was not until the cars had been unloaded from the transporter at Zandvoort that Clark had a chance to see the 49 in all its glory. Graham Hill had been allotted chassis #49/1 and Jimmy chassis #49/2.

By this point in time, Clark had driven for Chapman for a number of seasons, and was aware that Chapman's cars were fast but had a tendency to be fragile; a feeling echoed by a number of other drivers over the years. Added to this the fact the cars were literally straight from the box untried, and one can imagine that both Jimmy and Graham were a little apprehensive.

Zandvoort had been the home to the Dutch Grand Prix since 1949, and is located near Haarlem on the Dutch coast – so close to the coast in fact that the circuit is surrounded by sand dunes, which, with gusty winds blowing off the North Sea, had a nasty habit of depositing a liberal coating of sand across the circuit. The sand, as they say, could get everywhere, and as well as making the track difficult to drive could also do damage to the engines, it could jam throttle slides as well as clog filters. But it was a picturesque setting and at that time quite different to other tracks which were set in forests, on public roads, disused airfields or in parks. Jimmy had his first taste of Formula 1 with team Lotus at Zandvoort in 1960 driving the Lotus 18, only to retire with gearbox problems. Innes Ireland went on to finish second.

For a new car and engine, debut races do not come any better than this, for Clark's winning average speed for the 1967 event was faster than the old lap record. As well as winning the race, Clark also set fastest lap for a new lap record for the circuit. It was a remarkable demonstration of superiority by both car and driver.

Practice, however, did not bode well for the race, for Hill's car was plagued by ignition related problems, and Clark's car suffered a collapsed wheel bearing, which limited his practice to just a handful of laps. Despite all this, Hill managed to capture pole by scorching round in a time of 1min 24.6 sec, which was a staggering six seconds quicker than the previous lap record. Clark, with his limited practice time, still managed to grab eighth on the grid, alongside Denny Hulme in his Brabham-Repco and in front of the two Ferraris of Mike Parkes and Chris Amon. The 1967 Dutch Grand Prix was not one of the most enthralling races, but deserves its place in this book because it was an epoch-making race which heralded a whole new era for Formula 1, beginning on that day; June 4, 1967.

Across the board there seemed to be very strong driver pairings, such as Hill and Clark in their Lotus 49s, Rindt, Rodriguez and Siffert with the Cooper-Maserati V12s, Brabham and Hulme in their Brabham-Repco V8s, Stewart and Spence with the best that Bourne could produce in the shape of the latest BRM H16s, and Amon, Parkes and Scarfiotti driving V12 Ferraris. The Eagle-Weslake V12s were to be driven by Gurney and Ginther, but Ginther had withdrawn. Surtees was driving the lone (and troublesome) V12 Honda. The rest of the field was made up of Chris Irwin in a Lotus-BRM V8 and Bob Anderson with a four-cylinder Brabham-Climax. Thus, 17 cars formed up on the dummy grid under grey skies, before taking their place on the grid proper for 90 laps of the dry but sand-swept Zandvoort circuit.

As the flag dropped, Hill and Brabham got the jump on Dan Gurney in his V12 Eagle, as the front row led the chase down to the first bend: Tarzan. Rindt and Clark had also made good getaways, and, by lap eight, were up to third and fourth places respectively, after Gurney had made an early stop with his engine running erratically. Slowly, a gap developed between the first six cars and the rest of the field; these six consisting of Hill, Brabham, Rindt, Clark, Hulme and Amon. Bruce McLaren had gone out early on the second lap following a minor accident.

The race just seemed to be settling down when on lap 11 Hill's engine died on him after having chewed up its timing gear, letting Brabham take the lead. The first five cars were now covered by a handkerchief, or, to be more precise, 3.2sec, and all going for it hammer and tongs. By lap 15 Clark started to make his move and just made it past Rindt as they completed the lap. By lap 16, Clark headed Brabham to lead the race.

The race was now beginning to take its toll on the machinery as Rindt's Cooper-Maserati had developed suspension problems and was gradually being caught and harried by Hulme's Brabham-Repco. Hulme made it past Rindt two laps later, and Rindt proceeded to slip down through the field after being overtaken by the Ferraris of Amon and Parkes. On lap 39 Rindt's teammate Pedro Rodriguez retired his Cooper-Maserati in the pits with gearbox trouble, only to be joined by Rindt on lap 41. Not a good weekend for the once all-conquering team from Surbiton, champion constructor in 1959 and 1960.

Clark was now drawing away steadily, although he didn't have things quite as under control as appeared to the outside observer. His clutch was giving trouble, and he had brake balance problems to cope with. On top of this, the throttle linkage was making it difficult to control the power output from the engine, which had a tendency to come in with a bang. Still he managed to make it look easy, and increased the gap to the chasing pack that was headed by Brabham, teammate Hulme, and Amon, who was pushing Hulme for all he was worth. Meanwhile, Parkes in the other Ferrari could not keep the pace, and would be lapped by the first four, as would the third Ferrari of Ludovico Scarfiotti by the end of the race. Still Clark pushed on, building and building on his lead, and by lap 44 had lapped Surtees. Surtees was having a dreadful race after having started from the third row of the grid, the Honda having spun at the Hunzerug due to jammed throttle slides.

Racing with Heroes

This, no doubt, courtesy of the local Haarlem sand. He called it a day on lap 73, and left for an early bath.

The BRMs of Jackie Stewart and Mike Spence were having mixed fortunes, with Mike going on to finish eighth, albeit three laps down on the winner, after having to nurse the car through the latter stages of the race with low oil pressure. Stewart, on the other hand, had to retire on lap 44, having lost most of his brake fluid after hauling himself up to fifth at one point.

And so the race ran out with Clark crossing the finishing line nearly half a minute in front of Brabham, who was in turn barely two seconds in front of Denny Hulme. Clark had won the race at a record speed of 104.4mph, having completed the 90 laps of the Zandvoort circuit in just 2hr 14min 45sec. Thus the first page of the first chapter of the long and successful record book of Cosworth was written, and who better than Jim Clark and Colin Chapman to write it, coupled with the illustrious name of Lotus. Just as the name of Coventry Climax had done previously, so Cosworth would go on to make Britain a leader in the world of motor racing, humbling greater names such as Ferrari, Maserati and Honda in the process.

Although it has now been more than forty years since we lost Jim Clark, his name and his superlative driving skills will long be remembered. Not just in Britain and on the circuits throughout Europe and Australasia, but also in America, where he showed in his success at the Indianapolis 500 what a true champion can do. It doesn't matter what car, which race track, or what the weather conditions: brilliance will always shine through. Unfortunately, Jimmy's brilliance shone all too briefly, like a super nova on the racing circuits around the world, but similarly, his light will continue to shine with the memories he left for years to come.

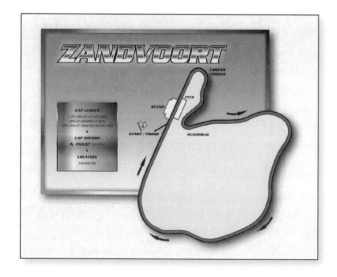

13 AUSTRALIAN GRAND PRIX – 1986

THE FICKLE FINGER OF FATE

AMID the flailing black remnants of what was his left rear tyre, and the shower of sparks spewing out from the dragging suspension and bodywork of the Williams, Mansell was wrestling with the car as it careered, barely under control, at nearly 160mph along the Dequetteville Terrace straight. The car yawed and slew from side to side on just three wheels as the weight transferred from front-to-back and side-to-side during its lurid high-speed dance along the black asphalt. It seemed to go on for an eternity before Mansell managed to bring it to a halt next to the barriers in the escape road. The cameras caught every spine-tingling second of it and anyone who witnessed it, on television or live, will surely not forget the sight.

The season's closing and championship-deciding Grand Prix was being broadcast live from Adelaide at some unearthly hour that Sunday morning, and as it was such a crucial race, I was seated in my favourite armchair well before the prescribed time of the race's start, together with my two sons, Stephen and Philip.

It was only the second Australian Grand Prix, counting for the Formula 1 championship as well as the last and deciding Grand Prix of the year for the 1986 World Formula 1 title, which was a three-way tussle between Nigel Mansell, Alain Prost and Nelson Piquet. Anyone of the three could clinch the championship, but fate would decide who the lucky one would be.

The mathematical probabilities were on Mansell's side, for he had 70 points, Prost had 64, and Piquet had 63. While the two Williams teammates (Mansell and Piquet) tussled throughout the year to win each race, Prost had been consistently gaining points as the season went by. By the time they reached Adelaide, Mansell had a six point lead over Prost, and was seven points ahead of Piquet, so it seemed that all he had to do was to make sure he finished in the top three placings, which shouldn't be too difficult for a driver of his capabilities.

During his career Nigel Mansell had become the fan's favourite, not only in this country but abroad. His no-nonsense hard-charging driving style won plaudits in Italy and the United States alike. In Italy while driving for the Ferrari team the Tifosi called

Racing with Heroes

him Il Leone; the Lion. In America when he won the Indycar Championship with the Newman Haas team, they accepted him as one of their own. In England, he stirred up Mansell-mania, when crowds invaded the circuit after his wins in the 1991 and 1992 British Grands Prix. He had many ups and downs in his career, which culminated in him winning the Formula 1 and US Indycar championships as back-to-back titles in 1992 and 1993 respectively.

For this race he would be driving his fabled 'red five' Williams, which he considered to be his lucky number. He had joined the Williams team in 1985 after having spent four years with the Lotus team and Colin Chapman, but after Chapman died Peter Warr had taken over the reins, and for Mansell things were not quite the same. Frank Williams spotted his potential and teamed him up with Keke Rosberg. Things got off to a slow start until the Belgian Grand Prix when he came second. This was followed by a win in the British Grand Prix, as well as the South African.

Although considered to be a hard-charging type of driver, it was also said that he needed the best car to be able to win. However, one can only admire and watch with awe some of the film footage of his overtaking moves, such as that in the 1987 British Grand Prix when he weaved from one side then the other to pass Nelson Piquet. Or that on Senna during the 1989 Hungarian Grand Prix, or his monumental pass around the outside of Berger at the Peraltada corner during the 1990 Mexican Grand Prix, which had the viewer hanging on to the edge of his seat.

For 1986, Keke Rosberg had moved to McLaren to partner Prost to drive the TAG powered MP4-2Cs, while Mansell was teamed up with Nelson Piquet, the Brazilian driver. To say that Mansell and Piquet did not get on would be putting it mildly. Since Piquet would be fighting his own corner, Mansell could not rely on any support during the coming race from that direction. Before the race, Rosberg, last years winner, had already said he would do whatever he could to help teammate Prost win the title. So although Mansell appeared to be the favourite, he was going to have to do it all himself.

One of the key factors for the race was going to be that of tyre wear. Now, it just so happened that both Williams and McLaren were using Goodyears, and so they would be monitoring very carefully one another's tyre wear during the race. The Goodyear technicians would also be keeping a close eye on the rate of tyre degradation to be able to advise the teams accordingly, for there was some speculation that the tyres may not last the full race distance.

During practice Mansell had taken pole, followed by Piquet, the Williams with their turbocharged Hondas obviously going very well on this circuit. They were followed by Senna in his Lotus, and Prost, and René Arnoux in the Renault, Gerhard Berger's Benetton, then Rosberg in seventh slot on the grid.

Shortly before the race the skies became leaden, and the threat of rain turned into reality. Out came the umbrellas as the drivers waited during the pre-race preparation on the grid. But the rain was not to last, and it petered out during the formation lap as the drivers wound their way around the dampened circuit to form up for the start. After a brief pause on red, the lights on the gantry went to green, and amid the hurly-burly they roared away from the grid, off down the straight and into the early afternoon sun. As they came round to complete their first lap, Mansell had already slipped to fourth place behind Piquet, Senna and Prost.

Piquet had got away to a flyer of a start, but it wasn't very long before he began to have fuel consumption problems and had to back off, letting Rosberg past. Not long afterwards, Senna's engine began to go off song, and he slowly slipped back through the field. Alboreto was out early on after having a coming together with Arnoux, and yet another previous World Champion, Alan Jones, had made it up to eighth place in the Lola-Ford before having to retire after just fifteen laps.

By now the slight dampness that had affected the track had disappeared completely. Prost was now pressing Mansell, and although he wasn't going to hand him his place on a plate, Mansell was not going to fight at this stage of the race – a race that he did not need to win. Perhaps he also had tyre wear on his mind and saw no reason to force the issue. Once past Mansell, Prost began to reel in Piquet, who then proceeded to spin on lap 23.

It was on lap 32 that the tapestry of events began to unfold, for it was on this lap that Prost picked up a puncture and was forced to head for the pits. It seemed his day was ruined and his dream of becoming World Champion in tatters. As his tyres were changed the Goodyear technicians checked them for wear and agreed that it was safe to let the teams know that the rate of tyre wear was not significantly high, and that one set of tyres would last the race ... but they were wrong.

Rosberg now had a big lead over the Williams pair, with Piquet taking second place at this, the mid-point in the race. Then it happened: on lap 63 Rosberg had stopped his car out on the circuit. The reason? A delaminated tyre. As soon as the news got back to the pits the Goodyear technicians were somewhat perplexed. It just so happened that Thierry Boutsen was also in the pits with tyre problems, and the decision was made there and then that the Williams pair should be brought into the pits immediately. But in racing, as in many things in life, timing is everything. The pit board was hung out immediately on lap 64 to bring the cars in.

It was then that Mansell, accelerating to top speed along the Dequetteville Terrace straight, found himself wrestling for all his life was worth to keep the blue and yellow Williams from spearing off the track into the concrete walls that lined the circuit at that point. It is testimony to his skill that he kept the car from touching anything that day, and to be able to stagger, ashen-faced, from the car; despairing of the chance that had slipped through his hands, but relieved to be able to fight another day. Say what you like about Mansell, he always gives it his all, and is certainly good entertainment value.

Piquet came into the pits to change his tyres and rejoin the race while Prost went on, reeling off the final laps, to win the race and the title. Had Prost not replaced his tyres, due to what turned out to be a fortunate puncture earlier in the race, he would have been in the same situation as the Williams duo, and the final result could well have been completely different. As it was, Alain Prost became the 1986 World Champion, and

Racing with Heroes

Mansell would have to wait another six years before being able to claim that particular crown, while Piquet went on to win his third world title the following season.

Since 1986 the venue for the Australian Grand Prix has changed from time to time from Adelaide to Albert Park, Melbourne, but is always a firm favourite with teams and drivers alike, thanks to the typically relaxed atmosphere and the enthusiasm of the Australian people. It has also changed its place on the calendar in recent years from being the last, to the opening Grand Prix of the season. But wherever and whenever it takes place, it often proves to be eventful.

14 A FAMILY DAY AT THE RACES

BRITISH GRAND PRIX – 1979

IT'S the eve of the British Grand Prix, this year being held at Silverstone, vying as it did on alternate years with Brands Hatch, to be the venue for this country's round of the International Formula 1 Grand Prix Championship series. A favourite time for many racegoers to make their way to the circuit, which lies among the quiet English countryside of Northamptonshire, in the small town of Towcester.

We are headed for the circuit in our trusty Triumph 1500, with boot and roof rack fully loaded with our four-berth frame tent and all the necessary kitchen and bedding equipment, not to mention food and drink and all the ancillaries to allow four people to be able to exist under canvas for two nights. The four people are myself, my wife, and our two young children, who are highly excited at the prospect of a weekend of camping, as well as going to see the British Grand Prix.

Even before we reach the outskirts of Silverstone, the giant hand of the ubiquitous advertising media has seemingly reached everywhere imaginable. In particular the blue and white colours of the Gitanes cigarette company stare down on us; from crane jibs, from haystacks, from the mountainous timbers of a sawmill, as well as hoardings on buildings. From time-to-time we have passed hitch-hikers along the road. Even into the late evening, they make their long, slow, painful trek to the circuit, relying on the generosity of the passing motorists.

As we near the circuit we find a group of a dozen or more campers resting from the efforts of their journey, some with backpacks that look large enough to contain all the comforts of home, including the kitchen sink. It seems to be more of a pilgrimage rather than a visit to a one day race meeting; there's a light festive spirit, even to the cars now forming a traffic jam nearly one and a half miles from the circuit entrance. Dusk is now drawing on as the night sky slowly darkens. Its a clear, cool summer's evening, but all that can be seen as we sit waiting are the tail lights of the cars in front, inching inexorably forward. As we creep nearer and nearer to the circuit, so the atmosphere becomes almost tangible. Now we can hear music, laughter, and people talking excitedly, as we approach a typical English country pub with its garden, bedecked with the not-so-typically English

Racing with Heroes

gaily-coloured umbrella-sheltered tables, and garden chairs and seats with predominantly young people spilling onto the pavement, many sporting the colours of their favourite team or their current idol. Some talk in loud, animated fashion, no doubt fuelled by the prospect of the forthcoming spectacle, but also by the local real ale. Others simply relax in the cool evening air, probably glad to take a rest from a long journey, and relieve the pent-up frustration of being caught up in the bumper-to-bumper crocodile that they had hoped to avoid.

Further along the steadily growing line of cars, at the turn-off for the circuit entrance, stands an apparently solitary policeman (resembling Canute of old), holding back the traffic from one direction to allow through-traffic to pass, and judging by the number of cars doing three-point-turns, just to join the end of the traffic queuing up from the other direction seems to be adding to the confusion rather than relieving it.

As we reach the junction we find the bastion of the law obviously revelling in his authority, for he has now stopped the flow of traffic from both directions for no apparent reason, and appears to be beckoning nothing but the evening shadows towards him. Then, cutting through the ever-increasing darkness, two shafts of light can be seen, accompanied by the deep-throated rumble of a heavy diesel engine, and slowly emerging out of the shadows comes a gigantic two-tier transporter, dwarfing all around it. As it passes, heading away from the circuit, we can see it's loaded with five of the sleek-looking BMW M1 cars, used in the one make pro-car championship series. These cars have been in action today in conjunction with the official timed practice session for Grand Prix cars, as a curtain-raiser for tomorrow's main event. The leviathan can be heard fading into the distance, making heavy work accelerating up through the gears, only to be followed by a second monster of similar proportions, trundling into the gloom on the relatively traffic-free side of the road.

At last we are in sight of the entrance turn-off. The driver of the car in front excitedly throws his arms in the air, then around the neck of his passenger. Slowly, we edge closer – we're here! Or, so it seems. Not wishing to overshoot the small branch road, we carefully ignore the policeman's signal waving us forward and gingerly turn left, following the bulk of the traffic in front. Still it's bumper-to-bumper, but at least we know that we're virtually there ...

Another twenty minutes and we are through the gates and being guided by the stewards. How much further?

It's a relief to finally be here, but frustrating to find that the queue of cars stretches as far as one can see, albeit across grassed fields and behind hedgerows now. We are, however, moving forward from one steward to another, and then another. The devious and sometimes hazardous route is cordoned off with roped-together stakes every so often. There seems to be a hold-up at the front of the queue just before it disappears behind a hedge; some drivers have got out of their cars and are talking to the stewards, so we stop again and wait. Some switch off their engines, some blip their throttles impatiently, while others just sit reading newspapers or magazines. There are always the odd one or two who haven't the patience to wait, or who simply can't see why they should have to wait and want to jump from the back to the front, completely oblivious to the dozens of people in front of them. From one corner of the field two motorbikes come buzzing out of the darkness in a mad dash to the far side of the field, and these are inevitably followed by others who think it a good idea.

The stewards continue to usher in the endless invading hordes, and slowly but surely we are directed to the area where we are to park and pitch our tent. As we come to a halt and put on the handbrake, we all breathe a sigh of relief – even our trusty stead. The children are eager now to get out and unpack the tent and get it erected. I just hope and pray that we have brought everything: in the past, we have been known to leave at home incidentals such as the frame poles! So, carefully we unload and start to put together the vital parts, but it's dark now, and by the light of torches and headlamps it is not easy to erect a four-berth frame tent, especially with two well-intentioned youngsters pitching in. Eventually it is complete, kitted out with cooker, pots and pans, and all the comforts of home. Well ... almost.

RACE DAY DAWNS

BY 11 o' clock we settle down for a good night's sleep to be ready for an early rise. No chance! Well after midnight we can still here people arriving, unpacking, setting up and, in some cases, partying into the night. Eventually all falls quiet, but no sooner it seems have our eyes have closed, than the throb of helicopters begins to fill the air, with dawn breaking in the east. The noise outside quickly increases as fellow campers avail themselves of the ablution facilities (which are fairly primitive), and make their way to the track, no doubt to get settled in a prime spot for the main event of the day, which is still a good few hours off. Some campers, on the other hand, make the most of an early start to get stuck into a hearty breakfast; either made by their own fair hand, or by wending their way to the numerous snack wagons and food and drink stalls that are already being uncovered and distributing their victuals to the ravenous masses. With two ever-hungry children – and since we had brought along the requisite kitchenware and food – we choose the former option. There is nothing quite like the smell and taste of freshly cooked eggs, bacon and sausages, eaten al fresco, to set you up for the day.

So, with the inner man fully sated, we clear away, collect everything we need for the rest of the day, and follow the ever-increasing flow of campers to the circuit, which is beginning to buzz with activity. We can see a never-ending flow of cars and pedestrians entering for almost as far as the eye can see. The predicted attendance figure is in the order of 100,000 spectators for today's meeting. As we get closer, the entire place is a wonderful splash of colour, as though an artist has dropped his pallet onto a canvas. People are decked out in the colours of their favourite teams or drivers, and some are draped in national flags or team flags such as the Tifosi's beloved black horse on yellow background that has become the Ferrari emblem. All of this against a backdrop of occasional white, fluffy clouds, lazily drifting across a bright blue sky above the vivid green of the grass in

Racing with Heroes

and around the circuit. From the stalls selling t-shirts, hats, sunglasses, ear plugs, posters, camera film, and all sorts of paraphernalia for the discerning fans, to those selling crepes, fish and chips, ice creams, hot dogs, burgers, doughnuts, confectionery, tea, coffee, soft drinks, and beer for the indulgent fans: the smells and colours are a sight to behold, and the atmosphere full of good humour and expectation. As well as the stalls, shops stocked with photographs, models, paintings and racing attire are inundated with customers that hardly have room to allow new browsers to squeeze in before others can exit, walking past, one can hear a dozen different languages and accents, including French, German, Italian, Spanish, Dutch, American, and even Arabic. Scouse, Geordie, Brummie, and Cockney accents of the mother tongue can also be heard. This is certainly a revelation to the children, who have not seen or heard anything like this before. They are excited and want to see everything that is going on, in spite of the almost sleepless night.

As the morning wears on and we can see and hear the cars appearing in the warmup sessions for the days races, it's time to pick our spot and settle before all the best positions become occupied. At last we find one close to the safety fence near Stowe corner; here we set down our picnic blankets and cool box, containing our lunch and drinks, to wait until things start to happen out on the circuit. No sooner do we sit down than one of the boys wants to go to the toilet. Luckily, one of the permanent blocks is not too far away, but as we get up to go, the BMWs we had seen on the transporters the previous evening are out on the circuit for their warmup, with some of the Grand Prix drivers on board. We proceed to watch these for the next ten minutes before carrying on our way. The crowds are really beginning to build up now, and in places it is a case of shuffling along shoulder to shoulder, as if we are in Petticoat Lane street market in London. Unfortunately when we get there, there is a queue nearly as long as the one at the ice cream vans, which are doing a roaring trade.

Eventually we return to our chosen spot to see the Formula 1 cars on the circuit for their morning session. The McLarens, Tyrrells, Williams, Ferraris, Arrows, and Brabhams etc are all there, resplendent in their team colours and sponsor's livery. They rasp their way around the circuit, one after the other. It is just possible to identify the drivers by their helmets. Although, in the case of the lesser known drivers, a quick look at the programme is needed to confirm the name of the driver ensconced in the passing projectile. At this point, people are rushing to the fences with their cameras to get a shot of the cars, prior to the hurly burly of the race, when it would be even more crowded and difficult to get a clear shot.

Before we know it, it's time for the supporting races to start, and sure enough, faithful to the timetable in the programme, the cars are beginning to form up on the grid for the first race. The commentary blares out from the numerous public address speakers dotted around courtesy of the voice that always sounds so familiar. One would swear it is the same voice at whichever racing event one attends – it is so unmistakably English and informed.

The racing continues through the morning and early afternoon with different formulae and categories, while the crowds, the heat, and the excitement are reaching a crescendo as the hands of the clock creep slowly towards the time everyone has been waiting for. The drivers, the teams, and grid positions have all been announced. All the marshals are at their respective stations. All the emergency vehicles are in place. The supporting races, the air displays, the massed bands; all have had their moments of glory.

We stand close to the safety fence to get as good a view as possible. There has been a last minute surge towards the fencing as we stand shoulder to shoulder in rows as best we can. It is crowded, but it is a good natured crowd, for everyone is here for the same reason – to witness this gladiatorial contest between the finest men and machines in this arena of speed, at the end of which there will be only one winner. Only one man will stand on that elevated top step of the podium clutching the winner's trophy. The toing and froing of the private planes and helicopters that has been going on since the early hours has almost ceased now, with only the odd one departing from the circuit as race time approaches.

Although from where we are standing we cannot see the start/finish line, we can hear the engine noise rise, and the commentary over the PA system suddenly becomes more animated. Everyone stands on tip-toe, cranes their neck, and waits to see the multicoloured blur that is the gaggle of 24 cars rush by as a howling, chasing pack. So quickly do they appear, then disappear from view, that the mind is left befuddled. It is possible to take in who is leading and possibly who is second, but because the cars are all so tightly bunched and jostling for position, there is little chance to take in any more. Perhaps next time around they will be a bit more spread out, and it will be possible to identify some of the others in the leading group.

Sure enough, as they flash past again after completing their first lap of the scheduled 68, a gap has developed between the leading bunch, containing Alan Jones in the Williams and Jean-Pierre Jabouille's Renault, before the rest of the cars, led by Clay Regazzoni, thunder past, with slight gaps between bunches of cars jousting for position. As they come through the corner on successive laps, some can be seen taking slightly different lines, and changing gears as they charge through, trying to muscle and harry their way past other cars that are slower but, for one reason or another, managed to make a better start. The sights, the sounds and the smells are intoxicating to the enthusiastic fans, few of whom will dare to take their eyes off the events unfolding before them.

Round and round they thunder for the first few laps until a pattern starts to settle, with gaps between various bunches of cars, each having their own race within the race. Unfortunately, someone has to be last, and there always seems to be one who has, for whatever reason, been in for an early pit stop and is now a lap down and trying to make up ground, but clearly lacks the speed, and seems to be slipping further behind on each successive lap. In the meantime, our two children are agog at the speed and sound of the cars as they pass by, and it takes me back to that first race meeting I attended at Crystal Palace nearly 25 years before. How things have changed.

The commentators, at different locations, continue to give out their constant stream of information, keeping the spectators updated on the events unfolding out on the circuit and in the pits. Unbelievably there are still throngs of people walking to and fro, either

Racing with Heroes

to find somewhere to answer a call of nature, or to find a better viewing point, or even searching for someone they intended to meet, or got separated from, in the chaos of the day. Why don't they sit down and watch the race? I can't understand it.

My wife, Marie, is trying to keep the lap chart, as well as answering questions our two boys fire off on a regular basis, while I attempt to take some 'action shots,' which will inevitably be blurred, out of focus, or contain only half a car. I cannot profess to be a second David Bailey, but by the law of averages, I must be able to get one or two half-decent snaps from a roll of 36 Kodak colour film on my little Olympus Trip camera.

As the race enters its middle phase the temperature gauge on Jones' car starts to rise, and within a few laps he has to pull out with an overheating engine, allowing Regazzoni to take the lead with Arnoux in hot pursuit in second place. There have been other changes behind them, and a number of retirements, including that of Niki Lauda, Mario Andretti and Nelson Piquet. The weather continues dry as the sun shines down on the Northamptonshire circuit, and the thousands of spectators bathe in the unexpected good weather. Even though the Grand Prix normally falls in the middle of July, good weather cannot always be counted on.

As we watch the race, it has already been a long day for the children, who are now getting hungry, and sure enough are making in-roads into the picnic lunch of sandwiches, chicken legs, sausage rolls, cakes and crisps, washed down by chilled soft drinks from the cool bag. As for me, I shall wait until the race is finished, as there is far too much going on the track to bother with eating.

In these closing stages of the race, Clay Regazzoni is reeling off the last remaining laps, the leading Williams is still looking strong, and continues with lowering lap times as the fuel load reduces and the handling of the car improves. The two cars at the front have now lapped the rest of the field, including a fast charging Jean-Pierre Jarier, who has fought his way past Watson up to third.

The chequered flag falls, signalling the end of the race as the leader flashes across the start/finish line to be followed a few seconds later by Arnoux in second place. Of the 24 cars that started the race, only 14 finish. Relative quiet returns to the circuit for a while; the winner has completed his lap of honour, the podium steps have been mounted by the first three finishers, and the trophies have been awarded, and the applause and cheers have died down. It is time for the last two supporting races to wind up the programme of events. Already some of the spectators are beginning to make their way to the exits, in an effort to beat the usual log-jam at the gates, as nearly 100,000 people start to make their divergent ways home.

For us there is no rush, as we will be staying another night to avoid the traffic queues, see the final races in comfort, prolong the under-canvas adventure for the children, and relax, rather than arrive home completely shattered. Eventually, with the spectators rapidly decanting from the stands and enclosures, we make our weary way back to the tent for a drink and supper before turning in, as other overnight campers start to strike camp before returning home.

A Family Day at the Races

As we awake on the Monday, everything is so different to the previous morning. Gone is the noise and clamour of race day. Gone also are the crowds, and the hustle and bustle. We rise, wash and breakfast in virtual tranquillity. Before we go, the boys want to have one last look at the track and the grandstands, but all that can be seen are the remains of the day before: the litter, the drink cans, the food wrappers, discarded programmes, promotional stickers etc. The stalls and food wagons have departed, the shops are shut; there is hardly any movement about the place. It all seems so empty, so hollow, so dead. Where 24 hours earlier, there was a buzz, a vibrant energy, an electric atmosphere; now there is a vacuum, a lethargy in the air, it's like a ghost town.

It is time to go, so we make our way back to the campsite, we pack our things away, dismantle the tent and load everything back into the car. We make our way to the exit, but as we do so we see one of our fellow campers taking his car out onto the circuit. This encourages one of the children to say "can we do that dad?" It seems like a good idea at the time, so we gingerly edge the car out onto the track. There is no one else going round, so off we go. With the car loaded to the gunwales we continue, but not exactly at racing speed. We try to follow the racing line through the corners, but the thing that strikes me is how difficult it is to see the apex of the corner due to the flatness of the circuit. How Jim Clark used to race and take the perfect line in the semi-prone seating position of the Lotus 25 doesn't bear thinking about. One lap is enough: just to say that I have done it is sufficient.

At last we find the exit and head off home, the boys waving at the rear window as we leave Silverstone far behind us, receding into the distance. Next year it will be Brands Hatch. Must get some tickets ...

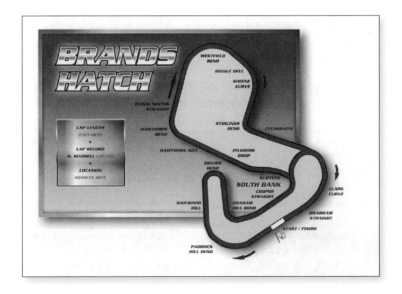

15 CANADIAN GRAND PRIX – 2011

THE FIRST SHALL BE LAST …

THE 2009 season was a momentous one for Ross Brawn, the Brawn Grand Prix team, and Jenson Button. It was to be their first, and their last, season in Formula 1. In that record-breaking year, the Brawn Grand Prix team had won the constructors World Championship, while Jenson Button had become the driver's World Champion.

For 2010, the Brawn GP team had metamorphosed into the Mercedes-Benz Grand Prix team, and Button had moved to the McLaren team to partner Lewis Hamilton. However, the general consensus of opinion was that this was not a wise move. Since 2007, it was known that the McLaren team was virtually built around young Lewis Hamilton, who had gone on to take the Formula 1 driver's crown in 2008 in only his second season in Formula 1. This followed Fernando Alonso's fractious season driving alongside Hamilton. Button was warned that he would be entering the lion's lair, and that it would not be easy. If those warnings unsettled Button, he never showed it.

Up to this point of the 2011 season, Button and Hamilton had been fairly evenly matched, although it would be fair to say that Hamilton generally qualified ahead of Button. The headlines the day after the 2011 Canadian Grand Prix simply read 'Brilliant Button' – it had certainly been an eventful race for him, but this is a massive understatement of what Jenson Button achieved that day, for just after halfway through this 70 lap race, he was dead last. He had two collisions, one with his teammate Lewis Hamilton, and one with the Ferrari driven by Fernando Alonso. He also suffered a puncture, made five pit stops and received a drive through penalty – hence his lowly position at the mid-point of the race. He then went on to make fastest lap on lap 69, then take the lead, and victory, on the last lap. Now that's what you call a hard day at the office! As he started to carve his way back through the field, most people thought the best he could achieve, perhaps, would be to pick up a point or two by coming home in ninth or tenth position. However there is more to this young man than meets the eye, for if he feels that things are going well, he sees no reason to settle for second place when first place is there for the taking. And boy did he take it, like candy from a baby.

Friday practice and Saturday qualifying had taken place in dry conditions, but the weather forecast for Sunday was not so promising. In the meantime, Vettel had made an uncharacteristic error on Friday, and crashed into the champion's wall. The Red Bulls initially didn't look to be in their normal dominating form, and the Ferraris and Mercedes were looking strong. At the end of Q3 however, the status quo had been restored, and the grid was headed with Vettel on pole and Alonso making up the first row, followed by Massa and Webber on row two, with Hamilton and Rosberg behind them, and Button and Schumacher in eighth position.

The race itself was a rather disrupted affair, due to the weather, and safety car interventions. The race actually started in fairly wet conditions, and the first four laps were run with the safety car. Then on lap 19, the heavens opened, and the race was red-flagged and not restarted until two hours later. The pattern for the day seemed to have been set.

Vettel had already won five of the first six grands prix of the season in Australia, Malaysia, Turkey, Spain, and Monte Carlo, and come second in China. Button's best result thus far had been his second place in Malaysia. His teammate Hamilton, in spite of having a win in China, was trailing Button by some 16 points – not quite what the pundits had predicted pre-season. It was going to be a long season, containing nineteen races and at the point of the Canadian Grand Prix it was not even halfway through, so there was plenty of time for a change in fortune for both McLaren drivers.

At the designated start time the predicted rain was falling heavily on the Montreal circuit, necessitating a start under the safety car which proceeded to lead the pack of twenty four cars around this 2.7 mile track for four laps before they were freed. Almost immediately, Hamilton tangled with Webber at the first corner, dropping the Australian to fourteenth spot and Hamilton to sixth. It seemed that Hamilton had his 'impatient head' on today, possibly frustrated with his poor practice position due to problems with incorrect gearing. Unfortunately, the same 'head' got him into more trouble later in the race, on lap seven to be exact, when he tried to overtake his teammate, who had slipped past, together with Michael Schumacher and Nico Rosberg, during Hamilton's earlier skirmish with Webber. The two touched after Button got out of shape entering the chicane: Hamilton jinked to the left, catching Button unawares as he stuck to the racing line, and squeezed Hamilton into the pit wall, who then caught the left rear of Jenson's McLaren on the rebound. The outcome of which left Hamilton with a deranged rear suspension. Not a particularly good start for either of them, and it was an incident that would require some explanation to Martin Whitmarsh, the McLaren team manager, after the race.

As Hamilton retired, Button made his way to the pits for a damage check on the car and to change tyres. This stop took place while the safety car was deployed because of Hamilton's damaged car. Button took this opportunity to take a gamble and to switch from the wets that he had started the race on to a new set of intermediates. There was a feint dry line developing, and Button was going to try to make the most of it.

Following the pit stop, he was back on track in 12th position behind the safety car that stayed out for another four laps on this occasion. The other teams were ready to monitor Button's times on the intermediates, but he now had to come in for a drive through penalty for excessive speed while the safety car was out. It seemed that Button's afternoon was going from bad to worse, and he still had that post-race embarrassing explanation to look forward to. Could he possibly redeem himself somehow?

It wasn't long, however, before the wisdom of switching to the Pirelli intermediate tyres began to pay dividends, for it was obvious both on the tack and on the stopwatch that Button was now beginning to make inroads into the lower orders, and he was now faster than the leader Vettel by a second a lap. It was this that made the Mercedes and Ferrari teams bring Rosberg and Alonso in from second and fourth places respectively to change to intermediates. But the Gods were in a museful mood that day, and by lap seventeen the rain started to descend again. As a result, Vettel and Massa stayed out on their wets, but Schumacher, bucking the trend, was brought in for inters.

With all this going on the likes of Kobayashi moved up to third, Webber fourth, Alonso fifth; followed by Heidfeld and Petrov in the two Renaults, and Paul Di Resta in his Force India. All was going well until lap 19, when the track was deluged by torrential rain which, unsurprisingly, brought out the safety car once again for six laps, until conditions became just impossible, and the race had to be red-flagged. During those six laps Alonso, Rosberg, Schumacher, and Button came in to change to wet tyres, and Vettel, Massa and Webber also pitted for fresh wets.

It was nearly two hours later before the race was able to get under way again, and once more it was with the safety car, which seemed to have covered almost as many miles as the race cars. The order at the restart was Vettel, Kobayashi, Massa, Heidfeld, Petrov, Di Resta, Webber, Alonso, De la Rosa, Button, Rosberg, and Schumacher forming the leading dozen. For nine laps the pack droned along behind the safety car before they were released once more. It was now lap 34 – nearly half distance. Vettel, as usual, made a good getaway, as Bert Mylander pulled the safety car off the track. The gap between Vettel and Kobayashi rapidly increased as Kobayashi fought a defending role to hold on to second spot. Meanwhile, Schumacher had charged straight into the pits as soon as the safety car had gone to change from the wets he and everyone else were on, back to the inters. The following lap, both Button and Heidfeld did the same. It was a gamble, but a worthwhile gamble that could pay off. Most of the rest of the field waited another two or three laps before making the move onto inters. It had certainly worked for Schumacher, for he was now up to seventh.

Alonso came out of the pits, only to be gobbled up by Button, who was now really getting his inters to work. Unfortunately, as Button was about to sweep past Alonso there was the merest of touches: enough to send poor Alonso spinning onto the adjacent raised kerb, on which the car became beached, and could only be moved by the aid of marshals, necessitating yet another safety car period. For Button it was another trip to the pits to replace a punctured tyre. Vettel also took advantage of the spell under the safety car to make his pit stop for inters without losing his lead. So, on lap 37 Button was last. What could he do now? In the words of the song, "the only way is up."

… AND THE LAST SHALL BE FIRST

O N this occasion Bert Mylander only had the safety car out for three laps before everyone was back up to full speed again. As before, Vettel led the way from Kobayashi and Massa, with the rest of the field in hot pursuit, all fighting for position with Heidfeld, Di Resta, Webber, Schumacher, Petrov et al, and Button bringing up the rear.

The one saving grace in Jenson Button's –up to now – unfortunate day was the regular appearance of the safety car, for each time Vettel had pulled out any sort of lead, it was negated. Even at this point in the race, although Button was last, he was not that far behind Vettel on the road. And so, Button started his meteoric drive that was to put him into the record books.

He carved his way through the field in scintillating fashion, passing cars on the inside and outside of corners, along the straights … in fact anywhere he could. His overtaking was not in any way dangerous or foolhardy, but precise and calculating. It was a pure joy to watch a master at work, especially in the changing and difficult conditions.

At the front Vettel was doing his usual masterful job of leading from the front and making it look easy. He was pulling away from Kobayashi at nearly half a second a lap. Kobayashi still had the close attendance of Massa, who couldn't find a way past in spite of being potentially faster. At this point, the track was still not fully dry. To attempt an overtaking move off the dry line was disastrous, as Di Resta found to his cost when he tried to overtake Heidfeld for fourth place. He effectively demolished his nose cone, which had to be replaced in the ensuing pit stop. Schumacher had squeezed past Webber after he made a slight mistake, and not only managed to keep Webber behind him, but also pulled a similar manoeuvre on Heidfeld which now put him up to fourth place. He now had his sights on Massa.

From the restart behind the safety car, Massa had a frustrating time behind Kobayashi. Try as he might, he just couldn't get past the Japanese driver in the Sauber-Ferrari. Kobayashi is never an easy driver to overtake, and in these conditions he made it impossible. In the meantime Button was pushing on relentlessly, and by lap 47 was up to 12th, and only 19 seconds off Vettel in the lead. With 23 laps still to go, Button was looking good for a handful of points. Kobayashi may not have realised it, but his pace was certainly doing Button a big favour. Button had Maldonado and Alguersuari in front of him but he quickly dispatched them with relative ease, and was soon hunting down the next pack of prey, now in sight.

It was about now that Massa tried a move on Kobayashi, for he had Schumacher breathing down his neck. This was arguably Schumacher's best performance since his return to Formula 1 in 2010. Unfortunately for Massa, as he tried to pass Kobayashi he couldn't quite make it, and as the two squabbled for second spot, Schumacher shot past the pair of them in a typical "Schumacheresque" move of old. The old fox was now in second, and looking good for a podium finish, or even a win if anything should happen to Vettel. Further back Webber, whose race up to now had nearly as many ups and downs as

111

that of Button, chose to take a chance on a set of super soft tyres, now a virtually complete dry line had appeared. Webber was going for broke, having made the decision, and was soon nearly three seconds a lap quicker than the leader. Button also spotted the potential, and made yet another pit stop at about the same time. These two were then followed by Schumacher, Massa and Heidfeld, all trying to cover one another's move in changing to the super soft dry tyres.

Phew! This was difficult to keep up with. It must have been a nightmare for those trying to keep their lap charts up to date! Montreal often produces a race filled with safety car appearances and incidents, and this one was no exception.

Massa was having the sort of race that he would rather forget, for after making his stop to change onto the dry tyres, he clipped the wall at Turn 7 and was soon back in the pits again for a new nose. He did, however, manage to climb his way back up to sixth by the end of the race, but a podium finish had definitely been on the cards until that incident.

With Massa now out of his way, Webber had climbed to fourth and was sitting behind Schumacher. It was now lap 53, and Vettel and Kobayashi came into the pits to change onto their super soft set of tyres. Vettel came back out with his lead in tact in front of Schumacher and Webber. Kobayashi and Heidfeld had been overtaken by the fast charging Button with just 15 laps to go, and Vettel was only nine seconds down the road and almost in sight.

Heidfeld was now on Kobayashi's tail, closing in for the kill; they were like a pair of WWII fighter pilots. Kobayashi did all he could in an effort to keep Heidfeld behind him. On lap 55 the inevitable happened, as when an irresistible force meets an immovable object. Heidfeld ran into the back of Kobayashi, wrecking his front wing and left the circuit, taking the escape road at Turn 3. It was time for safety car appearance number six, while the detritus was cleared from the track. Again Button gained from this five lap period, and again Vettel made a very competent job of the restart, leaving Schumacher and Webber to resume their battle for second place with Button ominously closing in.

The laps were now running down, and it felt that the remaining drivers were jostling for position, prior the last lap dash to the line. On lap 63, Webber tried a move on Schumacher at the chicane. It didn't quite work out and he went straight across the chicane, exiting in front of Schumacher, and as a result was obliged to give the position back. Not to be outdone, he tried again the following lap, but this time he didn't regain the track quite as readily and before he new it, he was looking at the rear of a McLaren. Jenson Button's McLaren, to be precise. Shortly afterwards, Schumacher's Mercedes wing mirrors were filled, also by Button's McLaren. You can't keep a good man down, it seems.

With 5 laps to go Button breezed past the Mercedes with his foot to the floor, DRS wing flap wide open, and KERS at maximum. Now things were getting interesting – what could Button do against the unflappable driving machine that Vettel had developed into during the course of the 2011 season?

He gave it his all.

Vettel was now just three seconds ahead of Button, with four laps of the race remaining. Button was now getting larger and larger in Vettel's mirrors. The one thing Vettel knew he must do was to stay at least one second ahead of Button, otherwise Button could deploy his DRS to maximum effect. Vettel now gave it everything he had and was lapping two seconds faster than before, but Button still grew larger in his wing mirrors.

On lap 69 Button was within the DRS trigger zone. Could Vettel hold on for just one more lap? Approaching Turn 6, Vettel, possibly distracted by Button's close proximity, put a wheel onto the wet side of the track. Suddenly the car whipped round as it oversteered out of the corner. Vettel calmly collected the car, got it back on line and carried on, but it was too late: in that instant, Button flew past and was on his way to taking the chequered flag.

While all eyes were on the action at the front, Webber finally forced his way past Schumacher at the chicane to come third, followed home by Petrov and Massa to complete the top six finishers. This was a race that will certainly be remembered by Jenson Button. Needless to say, the incident with Lewis Hamilton was put to one side amidst the euphoria of such a sensational victory.

16 JAPANESE GRAND PRIX – 1976

IN THE SHADOW OF MOUNT FUJI

IT was earlier than I would normally rise on a Sunday morning, but I cannot now remember what the hour was as I sat up in bed listening to a recount of the 1976 Japanese Grand Prix on the radio. It was the last Formula 1 Grand Prix of the season which brought the curtain down on an incredible year of emotional ups and downs, as well as judicial twists and turns before the outcome of the championship was finally determined. For throughout the 1976 season, a titanic struggle had developed between Austria's Niki Lauda and England's James Hunt. Unfortunately, the season had been somewhat overshadowed by technical infractions, team objections, driver penalties, disqualifications, and point deductions, which seemed to rumble on from one race to the next. There had also been that terrible accident of Lauda's that left him with horrific scars from the burns he suffered, although the outcome could have been a lot worse, as Niki's life hung in the balance in the hours that followed. However, being the determined kind of person he is, his rapid recovery meant that he only missed two grands prix before he was sitting in his Ferrari on the grid at Monza, for the start of the Italian Grand Prix.

The Japanese Grand Prix took place in atrocious weather conditions, with mist and rain making even the impressive Mount Fuji, which looms over the Fuji Speedway circuit, almost disappear at times. True to form for the 1976 season, drivers argued with race organisers and team managers alike that the conditions were impossible, and too dangerous to race. It got to the point where the dissenting drivers were virtually ordered to get into their cars and race. It was now October, and everyone would be glad when this season came to an end. Hopefully by the following year, sanity would be restored.

The situation in the championship was that if Hunt came no lower than third in the race, he would clinch the driver's title, as Lauda, the current World Champion, had just a three point lead coming into this, the final race, after having missed the Austrian and the Dutch Grands Prix. It was not going to be an easy race, for there were also drivers of the calibre of Mario Andretti, Ronnie Peterson, Jody Scheckter, Clay Regazzoni, John Watson, and Alan Jones on the grid.

Andretti was at the top of the sheets following the final practice session to give him pole position on the grid for the race. Hunt had managed to plant his McLaren alongside him on the front row, with Lauda in third and Watson in the Penske-Ford PC4 next to him, followed by Jody Scheckter's six-wheeled Tyrrell P34 and the Brabham BT45 of Carlos Pace. Next up came Clay Regazzoni in the second Ferrari, and the March of Vittorio Brambilla, sometimes affectionately known as the Monza Gorilla (a possible reference to either his aggressive handshake or his driving style).

During the delay prior to the start, the rain had been pretty persistent and the sky overcast. It was well into the afternoon now, although the sky gave no clue as to the time of day. Today dusk would come early, and the race would need to be started soon to prevent the finish taking place in very poor light as evening closed in. The Fuji Speedway was a scene of depressing mist and rain. It was the sort of day that if you were at home, you would think about going back to bed, or at least of staying within the warmth and comfort of home, and not venturing out into the cold and damp outside: the sort of day when, militarily, it would be a good time to commence battle – when your enemy were least expecting it. It was certainly going to be a battle, a battle of nerves, guts and tactics, when Hunt would need to screw his courage to the sticking place, if he were to achieve his life-long ambition. But all that could be seen around the circuit were huddles of umbrellas of different shades and colours in the stands, in the terraces ... everywhere, in fact, and behind those umbrellas were spectators, some of whom had been there since the early hours, in their Kagools and waterproofs of all descriptions. It was not a good day to go motor racing, for drivers or spectators, who were beginning to get restless (due partly to the orchestration of McLaren's team manager Alastair Caldwell) for the race to get under way.

GORILLA IN THE MIST

The field surged away from the grid just after three o' clock in the afternoon, one and a half hours after the programmed starting time. Hunt shot into the lead with one thing in mind; to get clear of the blinding ball of spray behind him, leaving the others to find their way round as best they could. For most, it was like a blind man trying to find his way around a room. They could hear the other cars all around, but could not see them, or the circuit. The track was still extremely wet, with rivers of water – inches deep in places – running across the track, as Hunt found out when he reached the right-hander after the start and almost lost control. Behind Hunt the drivers were inevitably cautious due to the low visibility. If some drivers were not happy before the start, their demeanour certainly had not improved after that first lap, for as well as the spray of rooster tails thrown up by the wide rear wheels, mist still hung cloyingly in the air as it had done for most of the day.

It was Watson in second spot behind Hunt, who was followed by Andretti on that first lap, but this was to change on lap two. For on the second lap Watson, blinded by the spray, ended up taking one of the escape roads, allowing Andretti up to second. It was at the end of the first lap that Lauda registered his protest and brought the car slowly into the pits, saying that the title was not worth killing himself for. He was not the only one, for Larry Perkins also called it a day on the same lap. Carlos Pace, another driver, did the same shortly after. Ronnie Peterson was also missing from the lap charts after the first lap, but in his case it was due to water on the electrics of the March. So, with barely two laps completed, the field was already reduced by four.

It was now Vittorio Brambilla who was on the march, if you will pardon the pun, for he had now managed to hustle his way past Andretti to claim second spot. He was revelling in the conditions, as he had done in 1975, to claim his maiden Grand Prix victory in the Austrian Grand Prix in a similarly weather affected race. He gradually worked his way to within striking distance of Hunt, and on lap 22 he had a go. He tried to pass Hunt on the inside of the left-hander, but Hunt shut the door. Not to be put off, he tried again at the next corner, but went in too deep, and in the still very difficult conditions the car got away from him and he very nearly collected Hunt's McLaren as he spun. For a moment Hunt could see a gorilla in the mist, but the spin dropped Brambilla too far back to cause Hunt any further concern. It was now Jochen Mass, Hunt's number two in the McLaren team, who had worked his way up to second. It must have given Hunt some degree of comfort to know that his teammate was riding shotgun behind him. From his lowly starting position of 12th on the grid, the young German had made very good progress through the field in such dangerous conditions. Unfortunately this only lasted until lap 36, when he became yet another victim of the treacherously wet track and spun, comprehensively demolishing the front of his McLaren. Next up to inherit his place was Patrick Depailler in his Tyrrell ... how long would he last?

Just after the halfway mark of this 73 lap race Hunt still led, followed by Depailler, Tom Pryce, Mario Andretti, Clay Regazzoni, Alan Jones, Gunnar Nilsson, Harald Ertl, Takahara and Jaques Laffite. But it was Pryce who was on the charge, and had been since the drop of the flag in an effort to elevate himself from his disappointing 14th grid position. By lap 39 he managed to dislodge Depailler from second spot and was really flying and looking good for a podium finish. It was this sort of performance that was beginning to showcase his undoubted talent behind the wheel. Unfortunately, that talent was to be snuffed out all too soon in a hideous accident at the Kyalami circuit in South Africa the following year, when a marshal carrying a fire extinguisher ran across the track into the path of Pryce's Shadow, which proved fatal for the pair of them. Pryce's luck was also about to run out in this race, as a mechanical failure forced him to forfeit his hard fought for second position. Another driver making his way through the ranks was Alan Jones in his Surtees-Ford, showing his future potential. The Australian would become Williams' first World Champion in 1980 with his hard-charging no-nonsense driving style.

The rain had now started to ease, and slowly but surely the track began to dry. A dry line started to appear around the circuit, albeit in patches at first. As the drivers were still on the heavily-treaded wet tyres on which they started the race, they began searching for the wet parts of the track in order to preserve them – except Hunt that is (this was in spite of signals from his pit advising him to do the same, for they were aware that at the rate he was going, he was going to destroy his tyres before the end of the race).

Predictably, as his tyres began to wear, so his pace began to drop off, allowing Depailler once more to close in on him. Then, in the course of two laps, he dropped two places. First, on lap 61, Depailler drafted passed him, then on lap 62 Andretti took advantage of Hunt's slowing McLaren. However, it wasn't long before Hunt was back up to second in this race of ever-changing conditions and fortunes, when Depailler pulled into the pits with a puncture, the tyre change dropping him to fifth place. This should have been a wake-up call for Hunt, and the McLaren team.

In the meantime Andretti was making the most of these developments to consolidate his position up front and control the race. On lap 68 Hunt's decision was made for him, when he too picked up a puncture. Luckily for him the tyre held out until just before entering the pit lane, when his left front tyre exploded. The smiles on the faces of the Ferrari mechanics in the neighbouring pit were all too obvious, for their man Regazzoni was now lying second. This was in stark contrast to the expression on Hunt's face as he sat in the McLaren cockpit fuming inside his helmet, for he felt that his team should have instructed him more positively regarding the rate of tyre wear, as they should have been monitoring the condition of his competitor's tyres. As soon as the car had come to a halt, the McLaren pit crew were all over the car, but it was now so low that they couldn't get the jack under it, which meant that they had to manually lift it on to the jack before the wheel could be changed. All of this was taking time; time which Hunt could ill afford to lose.

He was soon back on the track, but unaware of what position he had rejoined the race. There were now barley five laps remaining: all he could do was simply drive as hard as possible and pass whatever appeared in front of him on the track.

Hunt was still furious with his team, and was now driving almost blinded – not with the spray, but with the red mist that had now descended behind the visor of his unmistakable helmet. He threw caution to the wind as he forced his car on through the still difficult conditions. This was James driving at his best (or his worst), for he was throwing the car into the corners and driving with utter abandon; nothing was going to halt his assault on those in front of him in the few remaining laps of the race. First he caught Alan Jones and flew past him almost as though he wasn't there, then shortly after came upon Clay Regazzoni, who offered no resistance at all and allowed Hunt into third place, although Hunt didn't realise this at the time. Ferrari had failed to renew Regazzoni's contract for the following season, and this was his ironic way of saying 'thank you,' together with a two-fingered salute as he passed his pit!

As Hunt started the last lap he could see Andretti and Depailler in front, but still didn't know whether or not he was in a position to claim enough points to become World Champion. Then suddenly, there it was: the chequered flag was being waved; it was all over. He cursed his team under his breath on the slowing down lap, for he felt sure he had failed in his year-long struggle to wrestle the champion's crown from Lauda's grasp. When he finally pulled into the pits he couldn't control his temper any longer, and as he removed his helmet a tirade of abuse was directed at Caldwell and McLaren's managing director, Teddy Meyer, for what he felt was their sheer incompetence. It was some time before they were able to convince him that he had finished third to earn those all important four points (bringing his tally to 69 points to Lauda's 68 points) that would make him the new World Champion.

It is also worth noting that during the course of the race, the fastest lap time was posted by the local driver Masahiro Hasemi in his Kojima-Ford on lap 25 with a time of 1min 18.23sec.

Just a few hours later Hunt was on the plane on his way home with the rest of the team. He was holding a yellow gorilla that Caldwell and Meyer had presented to him after the race. He was now more relaxed and somewhat relieved. As he sat smiling and talking to his team, one wonders whether he thought, that after all the earlier post-race judgements of this tumultuous season, (such as that after the British Grand Prix), if it was still possible for the title to be taken from his grasp at the last moment.

Although he was glad to have won the title in 1976, James openly stated later that he felt sorry for Niki Lauda, and that it was a pity the title could not have been shared between the two of them, bearing in mind everything that the pair of them had been through during the course of the season. Lauda, however, would be back to claim another title – but not so James Hunt, whose life seemed to reach a pinnacle with this triumph; he was never quite the same person afterwards.

17 HE RACED WITH HEROES

THE QUIET MAN

IT is every motor racing fan's ambition to race, and if possible compete against their heroes, whether that hero is Fangio, Senna, Schumacher, Button, or whoever. Unfortunately for most of us this dream remains exactly that: just a dream, a mere fantasy. But for some who are perhaps more driven, or fortunate enough to be in the right place at the right time, it can become a reality.

One such person is an acquaintance of mine by the name of Bob Cook. He can be seen most Sundays at St Peter's Church in Sible, Hedingham, sitting in his usual pew, head bowed. Behind that laidback attitude and soft smiling face lies another visage, however: that of Bob Cook the racing driver of yesteryear. Even after all these years, the glint is still there in his eyes, and enthusiasm for the sport still courses through his veins.

Bob Cook, 'the gentleman racer.'

Racing with Heroes

He was born in Colchester, the son of a flour mill director. His father had intended for Bob and his younger brother to follow him into the business, but Bob had other ideas. He went on to study engineering with Davey Paxman in Colchester before pursuing a career in the motor industry, not only in Colchester but also Ipswich, Derby, and Canterbury during his early racing years.

Bob was fifteen years old when he went to see his first motor race at the Boreham airfield circuit in Essex, which left a lasting impression on him. It was also the first track that he raced, driving the 1.5 Riley for Dick Hardman. Unlike many drivers, racing did not run in his family, it was a bug that had got into his blood and simply stayed there. He started his racing career in 1952, the same year that the young Princess Elizabeth became Queen Elizabeth II of England. Driving a Riley Merlin 1.5, he was quick even then, and came to the attention of the local racing fraternity. He carried on racing through the 1950s, '60s, '70s, '80s, and '90s, up to the millennium. Over the course of five decades Bob drove pretty much all the circuits of England as well as Zandvoort in Holland and Spa-Francorchamps in Belgium. He drove various makes and types of car during that time including Jaguar XK120, Riley, Morgan, Cooper, Ginetta, and the D-type Jaguar. He also drove the unique Appleton special – a modified Maserati chassis with a blown Riley engine – a car first put together by RJW Appleton. He competed against such illustrious names as Archie Scott Brown, Mike Hawthorn, Stirling Moss, Jack Brabham, Eric Brandon, Ivor Bueb, Innes Ireland, and many more; getting some very impressive results in some instances, in spite of not having driven for the major teams. Most events that Bob took part in were national or club races organised by the likes of the 750 Motor Club and the British Racing & Sports Car Club. He enjoyed the long distance races, and was paired with Ivor Bueb for just such an event at Snetterton. His trophy cabinets at home are stacked full of cups and trophies of all sorts, reflecting the success he had at his chosen art.

But Bob is a modest man, and it is not until you start talking with him on his favourite subject of motor racing that he reveals the passion that made him the winner that he was on the circuits. During the long course of his racing years he had one or two minor accidents, nothing more. In fact, the only real accident he had was one that seriously threatened his life, after he crashed his motorbike and collided headfirst with a telegraph pole when a stray dog ran into his front wheel.

He had his share of offers – one to drive for John Cooper – but the logistics of travelling from Canterbury to Surbiton on a regular basis, as well as carrying on with his everyday work as a mechanic, was, he felt, too much. Bob was indeed a qualified mechanic, and a very good one at that, and it was in this capacity that Colin Chapman also approached Bob with an offer to become service manager. Unfortunately on the day that Bob arrived for the appointment made by Chapman, Chapman didn't appear for the interview, which left Bob less than impressed, and he subsequently walked away from the deal!

On the subject of other drivers, Bob feels that Fangio was the best, with his unruffled, precise-to-the-millimetre way of driving. He also feels that Jim Clark was unmatched for his naturally gifted driving talents, which he could adapt to pretty much any car he was given to drive, and within a few laps drive it faster than anyone else had been able to previously. In the case of the Lotus Cortina, he had even been known to literally drive the wheels off it!

Bob had a number of successes at Snetterton, which was, and still is, one of his favourite circuits. He knew well Oliver Sear, who was instrumental in the early days of the circuit in coordinating the organisation of all parties concerned, and was one of the stalwarts at that time and in the years to come.

During his years of racing Bob always had a full time job in the auto business. Even now, although he is in his late seventies, Bob still frequents such events as the British Grand Prix, the Goodwood Revival, Le Mans, and the motor cycling TT series of races on the Isle of Man, but now only as a well-informed, but still enthusiastic, spectator – still maintaining his links with the people he has befriended within the sport over the years.

The only regrets that Bob has after five decades of racing are that he never got to drive a BRM, a car for which he obviously has a lot of regard and admiration for. His other regret is that he never drove at Le Mans during his early years, but other than that he has thoroughly enjoyed his years behind the wheel and is rightfully proud of his achievements.

One of his treasured memories is that of driving with Ivor Bueb (the 1955 and 1957 Le Mans winner) in the D-type Jaguar at Snetterton. This was during what Bob fondly remembers as a golden era of racing in the 1950s and '60s, also considered by some to have been among the most dangerous periods. One of Bob's prized possessions is a Michael Turner picture of Archie Scott Brown driving the Lister-Jaguar in the only way that Archie knew how, which hangs proudly on the wall of his house in his quiet north Essex village.

Another racing friend of Bob's was Lord Patrick Lindsay, frequently pictured driving a 1.5 ERA often referred to as Remus (one of the Romulus and Remus pair of ERAs), at various circuits. Coincidentally, his son, Jason Lindsay owns the De Vere castle in Castle Hedingham in the neighbouring village to Sible Hedingham, where Bob lives.

Bob's more recent successes were with his Ginetta G4, and included class wins in kit-car races, sprint wins, and making fastest time of the day at Snetterton during 1982 together with a championship win.

To a large extent, Bob has lived and fulfilled his dream: he has raced with his heroes, and unlike a lot of them has survived to tell the tale. He is still very much in love with the automobile, and currently runs a Mercedes SL500, has two Ginettas, a Citroën C6 and his Riley Merlin.

Many fans of motor racing, including myself, would have given their right arm (though this might not have been a good career move!) to have achieved what Bob has throughout his racing life. From his marriage Bob has two sons, who grew up during his years of racing, and he was fully supported by his wife the whole time until, sadly, she died of bone cancer.

It is the likes of drivers such as Bob, who form the basis and grassroots of motor racing, and have done over the years to put this country in the vanguard of the sport. It

Racing with Heroes

is thanks to people like Bob that motorsport in the UK has progressed from a time when Britain was almost considered a joke – particularly by countries such as France, Italy and Germany which, with the likes of Renault, Itala and Mercedes-Benz, led the field in motoring – to the present, when the majority of Formula 1 design and construction is carried out here. Added to this, the number of quality circuits that exist in the UK, together with the various competitions in a multitude of different formulae that take place here, has made for a healthy state in UK racing in recent years. Apart from the likes of Bentley, Sunbeam, Riley and one or two other manufacturers, British success in motor racing was very limited in the early days. Then along came ERA, with its ventures into voiturette racing in the hands of Raymond Mays, Reg Parnell and Prince Bira, which led to the formation of BRM and, subsequently, Connaught and Vanwall. The rest, as they say, is history.

It can only be hoped that one day Bob will write his own book about his fifty years of experiences in the world of motor racing, for it is sure to be a treasure trove of memories, anecdotes and stories that would make a good read, and be worth a few pounds of any enthusiast's money.

Through the years that Bob raced, he did so without the acclaim and the high financial rewards that are currently paid to some in the racing fraternity. He raced for the love of it, and for the challenge of competing against the great drivers of the time. Some, considered to be great drivers, were not necessarily great people, while for others the opposite could be said – but then this is true in all walks of life. For Bob, racing was simply a challenge that he rose to and thoroughly enjoyed.

Heroes are varied and come in all shapes and sizes; with their underpants worn over their tights, or as a Clint Eastwood-like character, or even a Formula 1 World Champion. Bob, for his part, not only raced with heroes, but, although one wouldn't think so to see him on a Sunday morning, was a hero himself.

And the sport still needs heroes like Bob Cook.

The Riley that Bob first raced at the beginning of his career.

Bob Cook in his Ginetta G4.

Also from Veloce Publishing ...

A unique collection of behind-the-scenes stories and anecdotes as told, in their own words, by former Grand Prix mechanics who have worked at the top level of the sport during the past 50 years.
On the front line of the sport, mixing with drivers and team bosses, they saw a side of it that nobody else got to see and rarely gets to hear about – and this book tells their story, supplemented by photographs from the archives and photo albums of the mechanics themselves, many of which are previously unpublished.
ISBN: 978-1-84584-199-7 • Paperback • 21x14.8cm
£12.99* UK/$24.95* USA • 176 pages • 89 colour and b&w pictures

For more info on Veloce titles, visit our website at www.veloce.co.uk
email: info@veloce.co.uk • Tel: +44(0)1305 260068
* prices subject to change, p&p extra

Also from Veloce Publishing ...

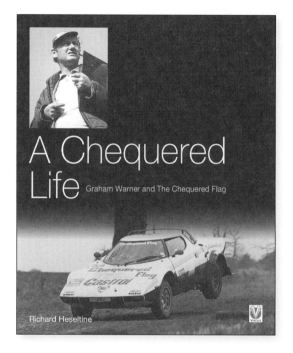

A Chequered Life
Graham Warner and The Chequered Flag

Richard Heseltine

This is the first and only account of the Chequered Flag race team and its charismatic founder, Graham Warner. It charts the highs and lows, the victories and losses, and features interviews with the man himself and several star drivers of the 1960s and '70s. Accompanied by 150 photographs, many previously unpublished, plus a look at Graham's subsequent career as a fighter aircraft expert and restorer, this is a unique story of a fascinating life in motorsport.

ISBN: 978-1-845844-13-4 • Hardback • 25x20.7cm
£30* UK/$49.95* USA • 160 pages • 140 colour and b&w pictures

For more info on Veloce titles, visit our website at www.veloce.co.uk
email: info@veloce.co.uk • Tel: +44(0)1305 260068
* prices subject to change, p&p extra

Also from Veloce Publishing ...

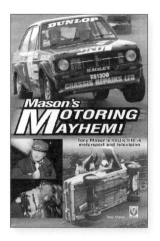

A full, frank and hilarious account of Tony Mason's hectic life, from humble beginnings in the Lake District to stardom on television and in motorsport. His story includes his business life, TV mistakes, rallying crashes, appearances on stage and travels to many far-flung places, all packed with laughs along the way.

ISBN: 978-1-845844-39-4 • Hardback
22.8x15.3cm • £24.99* UK/$49.95* USA
208 pages • 123 colour pictures

Nigel Bennett's unique autobiography describes his life and career, from growing-up influenced by car design, to his education and the building of his 750 specials. He describes his work as Firestone Development Manager, recounting many tales of the outstanding designers and drivers of the period. Detailing his work in Formula 1, as a Team Lotus engineer, and then as Team Ensign designer, he also covers his Indycar designs at Theodore, Lola Cars and Penske Cars. Life after his retirement, his involvement in boat design and with modern F1 teams, are also recounted.

ISBN: 978-1-845845-36-0 • Hardback • 25x20.7cm
£35* UK/$54.95* USA • 176 pages • 194 colour and b&w pictures

For more info on Veloce titles, visit our website at www.veloce.co.uk
email: info@veloce.co.uk • Tel: +44(0)1305 260068
* prices subject to change, p&p extra

INDEX

A
Abruzzi 51
Achilles 54, 61
ADAC Eiffelrennen 19
Adelaide 97, 100
Adenau 20
Adriatic 51, 53
Ahrens 34
Aintree 20
Albert Park 100
Alboreto, Michelle 99
Alfa Romeo 10, 13, 15, 59-61
Alguersuari 111
Allison, Cliff 27, 28
Alonso, Fernando 10, 37-41, 108-110
Amon, Chris 63, 81, 82, 94, 95
Anderson, Bob 95
Andretti, Mario 12, 93, 106, 114-117
Apennine 51
Appleton, RJW 120
Appleton Special 120
Aquila 54
Ardennes 18
Aremberg 23
Argentina 19
Arnoux, René 98, 99, 106
Arrows 104
Ascari, Alberto 13, 14, 16, 58, 62
Ascari, Antonio 13, 50
Aston Martin 16, 31
A Story of Formula 1 15
Attwood, Richard 33, 34
Audi 15, 31
Austin Healey 32
Autocar 15
Automobile Club d' Italia 62
Autosport 15
Auto Union 18, 58-60
Avus 47

B
Baghetti, Giancarlo 25, 88, 89, 91, 92
Bailey, David 106
Balestrero 60
Bandini, Lorenzo 89
Barnard, John 84
Barrichello, Rubens 39
Barth, Edgar 19
Baxter, Raymond 15
Bayardo 44
Behra, Jean 15, 16, 19, 43-46
Belgium 18
Bell, Derek 10, 12, 31, 32, 35
Beltoise, Jean-Pierre 35, 63
Benetton 98
Bentley 31, 122
Bentley Boys 31
Berger, Gerhard 98
Berthon, Peter 63
Bianchi, Lucien 89
Biondetti 50
Bira, Prince 122
Blackwall tunnel 9
BMW 102, 104
Bologna 51, 52, 56
Bolster, John 15
Bonnier, Jo 26, 28, 29, 43, 45, 63,

88-92
Bordeaux 49
Border Reivers 93
Boreham 120
Bourdais, Sébastien 39, 40
Bourne 95
Boutsen, Thierry 99
Bow 9
Brabham 10, 94, 95, 104, 115
Brabham, Jack 15, 16, 19, 25, 27, 28,
43-45, 89, 91, 95 120
Brambilla, Vittorio 115, 116
Brands Hatch 10, 82-85, 93, 101, 107
Brandon, Eric 120
Brawn, Ross 108
Brescia 49, 50-57
British Racing Partnership 43
BRM 10, 15, 16, 26-29, 43-45, 47, 63,
64, 81, 82, 88, 89, 92, 95, 96, 121, 122
Broadley, Eric 32
Brooks, Tony 20, 26, 28, 29, 43-47, 89
BRSCC 10, 15, 120,
Bueb, Ivor 15, 120, 121
Buenos Aires 46
Bugatti 15, 60
Buonarroti, Michelangelo 55
Burgess, Ian 89
Button, Jenson 39, 108-113, 119

C
Caldwell, Alastair 115, 118
Campbell, Malcolm 12
Canestrini, Giovanni 49
Canterbury 120
Canute 102
Caracciola, Rudolf 18, 50, 59-62
Casino Square 25
Castagnetto, Renzo 49
Castel d'Ario 58
Castellotti, Eugenio 50, 52-54
Castle Hedingham 121
Cevert, François 63, 64, 81, 82
Champcar 13
Chapman, Colin 12, 93, 94, 96, 98,
120
Chagall, Marc 89
Chenard & Walcker 31
Cheshire 47
Chevron 82
Chiron, Louis 28
Citroën 121
Clark, Jim 12, 14, 26-28, 47, 60, 89,
91-96, 120
Colchester 120
Collins, Peter 18-20, 22, 23, 59
Collombe 89
Colosseum 83
Connaught 47
Continental 19
Cook, Bob 119-122
Cooper 10, 15, 16, 19, 26, 27, 29, 43,
44, 46, 47, 88-90, 92, 95, 120
Cooper, John 120
Copersucar 84
Coppuck, Gordon 84
Costin, Mike 93
Cosworth 93, 96
Coulthard, David 39
Courage, Piers 35

Coventry Climax 25, 26, 89, 96
Cowell, Simon 11
Cremona 51, 56, 57
Crystal Palace 9, 10, 105
Curva Grande 64, 81

D
D-type Jaguar 121
d'Orey 44, 47
Daimler-Benz 57
D'Annunzio, Gabriel 58
Davey Paxman 120
Davis, Colin 43
de Beaufort, Carel G. 19, 44, 47, 89
Dennis 9
Dennis, Ron 12, 37, 38, 40
Depailler, Patrick 116, 117
Dequetteville Terrace 97
Derby 119
De Tomaso 89
Deutschland 18
De Vere 121
DFV 93
Dingle Dell 85
Di Resta, Paul 110, 111
Donington 58
Druids 86
Duckworth, Keith 93
Dukinfield 47
Dundrod 50
Dunlop 33
Duns 93
Dutray 33

E
Eagle, Weslake 12, 95
Eastwood, Clint 122
Ecclestone, Bernie 14, 22, 38
Eifel 18, 19
Eiffelrennen 18
Elford, Vic 33-35
England 19
Englebert 20
Epsom 63,
ERA 60, 63, 121
Ertl, Harald 116
Esses 39, 40
Essex 119

F
Fagioli 60, 61
Fangio 12, 13, 15, 16, 18-23, 25, 27,
32, 37, 46, 50, 52, 56, 59, 62, 63,
90, 119
Farina 62
Ferrara 53
Ferrari 15, 16, 19, 20-22, 26-30, 31, 32,
38, 42, 44-46, 50, 52, 57, 59, 60, 62-
64, 81, 84,- 91, 92, 95-97, 104 108,
109, 114, 117,
Ferrari, Enzo 56, 58, 62
FIA 14
Fiat 50, 56
FISA 89
Fisichella (Fisi), Giancarlo 39, 40, 41
Fitch, John 57
Fittipaldi, Emerson 64, 84
Flockhart, Ron 43-46
Florence 51, 52

Flugplatz 18
Force India 110
Ford 31, 32
Ford GT40 32, 34, 35
France 19
Francis, Alf 12
Fuji Speedway 87, 114, 115
Futa 56

G
Ganley, Howden 63, 64, 81, 82
Gasworks Hairpin 25, 28
Gendebien, Olivier 31, 43-46
Gessel 57
Gethin, Ken 63
Gethin, Peter 63, 64, 81, 82
Geux 88, 89
Giambertone 21, 22
Giardini 57
Gibson 19
Ginetta 119, 121
Ginther, Richie 26-29, 89-91, 95
Gitanes 101
Glock, Timo 39, 40, 41
Godia 19
González, Froilán 63
Goodwood 10, 12, 16, 25, 121
Goodyear 98, 99
Gould 19
Gregory, Masten 19, 23, 43-45
Grimaldi 25
Guichet, Jean 35
Guildford bypass 23
Gurney, Dan 15, 26, 28, 43-45, 88, 89, 91, 92, 95

H
Haarlem 94, 96
Hailwood, Mike 35, 63, 81-83
Halford, Bruce 19
Hamilton, Lewis 11, 37-42, 108-110, 113
Hantzenbach 18
Hardman, Dick 119
Harry Flatters 64, 81
Hasemi, Masahiro 118
Hawthorn, Mike 18-23, 31, 44, 59, 83, 90, 120
Heidfeld, Nick 110-112
Hermann, Hans 19, 26-28, 34, 35, 50, 56
Hesketh, Alexander 83, 84
Hill, Graham 10, 14, 16, 25-28, 44, 45, 63, 89, 91-95
Hill, Phil 10, 26, 28, 29, 43-46, 89-91
Hitler, Adolf 49, 61
Hobbs, David 35
Hocheichen 18
Honda 95, 96
Horsley, Bubbles 83
Hotel de Paris 25
Hulme, Denny 84, 94-96
Hunt, James 10, 12, 83-87, 114-118
Hunzerug 95

I
Ickx, Jacky 10, 31-35, 63, 64, 81
Il Leone 98
Indianapolis 27, 28, 93, 96

Indycar 98
Interlagos 38
Ipswich 120
Ireland, Innes 14, 15, 27, 44, 45, 91-93, 120
Irwin, Chris 95
Isle of Man 121
Italy 122

J
Jabouille, Jean-Pierre 105
Jaguar 9, 15, 16, 31, 120
Jarama 94
Jarier, Jean-Pierre 106
Jenatzy, Camille 12
Jenkinson, Denis 12, 14, 16, 50, 51, 52-57, 64
Joest 35
John Player 86
Jones, Alan 86, 99, 105, 106, 115-117
Junção 41

K
Karrusel 18
Kelleners 35
Kentagon 10
Kilmany 93
Kling, Karl 50, 55
Kodak 106
Kobayashi 110-112
Kojima-Ford 118
Kovalainen 39
Kristensen, Tom 31
Kubica, Robert 39
Kyalami 116

L
Laffite, Jacques 86, 116
Lagache, André 31
Lancia 19
Larrousse, Gérard 34, 35
Lauda, Niki 10, 12, 13, 84-87, 106, 114-116, 118
Lausitzring 13
Lautenschlager 12
Léonard, René 31
Le Mans 13, 15, 28, 31, 35, 50, 93, 121
Levegh, Pierre 31, 32, 50
Lewis-Evans, Stuart 19, 20
Ligier 86
Lindsay, Jason 121
Lindsay, Lord Patrick 121
Lins 34
Lister-Jaguar 121
Lola 32, 99
Lombardy 51
London 104
Lord's Taverners 87
Lotus 10, 15, 16, 26, 27, 29, 30, 43, 47, 64, 88, 89, 91, 93-95, 98, 107
Lotus Cortina 93, 121

M
Madrid 31, 49
Maggi, Aymo 49
Maglioli, Umberto 19, 50, 57
Mairesse, Willy 89
Maldonado, Paster 111
Mansell, Nigel 10, 62, 97, 98, 99, 100

Mantovano 58
Mantua 51, 57, 58, 60
Maranello 30, 45
March 63, 83, 86
Marcia Reale 61
Marie 10
Marimón, Onofre 23, 62
Marko, Helmut 63, 64
Marquis de Portago 49
Marsh 19
Martini 25
Marzotto 50
Maserati 10, 15, 19, 20, 22, 23, 29, 31, 44, 45, 50, 56, 57, 59, 96, 120
Massa, Felipe 38-42, 109, 111-113
Mass, Jochen 84, 116
Matra 32, 35, 63, 81
Matra Simca 63
May, Michael 26-28, 89
Mays, Raymond 12, 63, 122
May, Stephen 97
Mazzotti, Franco 49
McLaren 15, 26, 29, 37, 38, 40, 41, 84, 85, 89, 91, 92, 98, 104, 108, 109, 112, 113, 115-118
McLaren, Bruce 26-28, 43, 44, 46, 95
Medici 55
Mercedes-Benz 15, 18, 32, 46, 50, 52-54, 56, 57, 59-61, 110, 112, 121, 122
Merzario, Arturo 86
Mexico City 94
Meyer, Teddy 118
Milan 49, 62, 88
Milanese 92
Mille Miglia 10, 11, 49, 50, 58, 59
Mirabeau 25
Modena 51, 56
Monaco 25-28, 89
Monégasque 25
Monte Carlo 27, 29, 83, 89, 109
Monteferrario 57
Monti, Flaminio 49
Montreal 112
Monza 10, 19, 38, 49, 62, 81, 82, 90, 115
Morgan 120
Mosley, Max 22
Mosport Park 94
Moss, Stirling 10, 12, 15, 16, 19, 25-30, 32, 37, 43, 44, 45-47, 50, 51-59, 63, 88-91, 120
Motor 15
Motor Racing 15
MotorSport 15, 50, 57
Mount Fuji 87, 114
Muizon 44, 90
Mulsanne 34
Murphy 63, 82
Mussolini 49
Musso, Luigi 19
Mylander, Bert 110, 111

N
Nakajima 39
Naples 88
Naylor 19
Nazi 61
Neubauer 18, 61
Newman, Haas 98

Nilsson, Gunnar 86, 116
Nivola 58
Noghès, Antony 25
Nordkehre 23
Nordschleife 18, 19
Northamptonshire 101, 106
Nürburg Castle 18
Nürburgring 18, 21, 23, 30, 59
Nuvolari, Arturo 58
Nuvolari, Elisa 58
Nuvolari, Tazio 13, 51, 57-62

O
Oliver, Jackie 33-35
Olympus Trip 106
Osca 89

P
Pace, Carlos 38, 115, 116
Paddock hill 85
Padova 51, 53
Panamericana 50
Paris 31, 49
Parkes, Mike 94, 95
Parma 56
Parnell, Reg 63, 122
Penske 86, 115
Peraltada 98
Perkins, Larry 116
Pescara 51-54
Pescarolo, Henri 63, 64
Peterson, Ronnie 62-64, 81-83, 93, 114, 116,
Petrov, Vitaly 110, 111, 113
Petticoat Lane 104
Philip 97
Piacenza 56
Pietsch, Paul 60
Pimms 25
Piper, David 14
Piquet Jr, Nelson 39
Piquet, Nelson 10, 97-100, 106
Pirelli 20, 110
Pista Magica, La 82
Ponte Vecchio 55
Popoli 54
Porsche 14, 19, 25, 31-35, 88-90, 92
Porsche, Ferdinand 58
Postlethwaite, Harvey 83
Pratt and Whitney 64
Prince Louis II 25
Princess Elizabeth 120
Prost, Alain 10, 97, 99, 100
Pryce, Tom 86, 116

Q
Queen Elizabeth 120
Quiddelbacher Höhe 18

R
Radicofani 55
Räikkönen 37-42
Rascasse 28
Raticosa 55, 56
Ravenna 51-53
Red Bull 39
Redman, Brian 33

Regazzoni, Clay 63, 64, 81, 84-86, 105, 106, 114-117
Regenmeister 60, 61
Reggio 56
Reims 31, 43, 88-90
Reinhold 35
Remus 121
Renault 32, 37, 40, 98, 105, 110, 122
Rhine 18
Riley 120, 122
Rindt, Jochen 10, 15, 62, 93, 95
Roche, Toto 44, 90
Rodriguez, Pedro 95
Rome 49, 51, 52, 54, 58, 83
Romulus 121
Rosberg, Keke 10, 98, 99
Rosberg, Nico 39, 109, 110
Rosemeyer, Bernd 18, 59, 60

S
Salvadori, Roy 15, 19, 43
Sao Paulo 38
Sarthe 31
Scarfiotti, Ludovico 95,
Scarlatti 19, 47
Scheckter, Jody 85, 86, 114, 115
Schell, Harry 15, 19, 43, 45, 46, 63
Schumacher, Michael 10, 11, 14, 109-112, 119
Schwalbenschwanz 22
Schwedencruez 18
Scott Brown, Archie 120, 121
Seagrave, Henry 12
Seaman, Richard 59
Sear, Oliver 121
Senna, Ayrton 10, 13, 14, 98, 99, 119
Shadow 116,
Sible Hedingham 119, 121
Sicily 25, 50, 92
Sienna 51
Siffert, Jo 33, 63, 64, 81, 82, 95
Sighinolfi 57
Silverstone 10, 83, 94, 101, 107
Snetterton 120
Sommer, Raymond 31
Southgate, Tony 63
Spa-Francorchamps 31, 59, 62, 90, 94, 120
Spence, Mike 95, 96
Sporthotel 20
Station hairpin 25, 29
Stewart, Jackie 10, 11, 12, 18, 59, 62-64, 95, 96
St Devote 25, 28
Stommelen, Rolf 33, 34
Stowe corner 104
St Peter's 119
Stuck, Hans 59-61
Stuttgart 57
Südkehre 21, 22
Sunbeam 122
Surbiton 95, 120
Surtees, John 12, 15, 26-28, 60, 65, 90, 95, 116
Sutil, Adrian 39
Swanley 83
Syracuse 47, 88, 90

T
Tabac 25
Takahara 116
Targa Florio 50
Taruffi, Piero 50, 54-56
Tarzan 95
Tavoni 21, 22, 91, 92
Taylor, Simon 15
Taylor, Trevor 89
Teutonic 18
Thillois 44-46, 90-92
Tifosi 62
Titans 18
Tourist Trophy 121
Towcester 101
Toyota 38, 39
Trintignant, Maurice 28, 43, 45, 47
Triumph 101
Trulli, Jarno 38-40
Turner, Michael 121
Tyrrell 63, 64, 85, 104, 115
Tyrrell, Ken 12

U
UDT Laystall 89
Uhlenhaut, Rudolf 18
United Kingdom 49

V
Vaccarella, Nino 35
Vandervell, Tony 19
Vanwall 10, 15, 19, 47
Varzi, Achille 58-60
Verona 51
Vettel, Sebastian 14, 39-41, 109-113
Via Emilia 56
Viale Venezia 52
Villeneuve, Jacques 13
Villoresi, Luigi 50
von Brauchitsch, Manfred 18, 59, 61
von Trips, Wolfgang 26, 28, 29, 62 89, 90, 91

W
Wagner 18
Walker, Murray 87
Walker, Rob 12, 26, 29, 30, 43, 45, 59, 82, 89
Warr, Peter 98
Watkins Glen 94
Watson, John 86, 106, 115
Webber, Mark 39, 109-113
Wellington 83
Whitehouse 33, 35
Whitmarsh, Martin 109
Williams 15, 84, 86, 97-99, 104-106, 116
Wisell, Reine 64
Wyer, John 33, 35

Y
Yardley 63
Yeoman Credit 29, 89

Z
Zandvoort 10, 83, 90, 94-96, 120
Zanardi, Alex 13
Zolder 86